THE INVISIBLE SPOTLIGHT

WHY MANAGERS CAN'T HIDE

Craig Wasserman and Doug Katz

ISBN: 1460926013
ISBN-13: 9781460926017
Library of Congress Control Number: 2011902623

TABLE OF CONTENTS

INTRODUCTION

Whether managers appreciate it or not, they are a central and dominant influence in their employees' lives. Employees spend countless hours watching, listening, thinking about, talking about, and trying to please their bosses. This is what we mean by the invisible spotlight. Being in that constant spotlight comes with the territory.

Because of the management position you hold – because of its status and authority – your words and deeds carry enormous weight. They can heighten your employees' commitment in a profound and lasting way. They can help your employees perform – and want to perform – at exceptional levels. By the same token, your words and deeds can cause your employees hours of uncertainty and distress – even the off-handed remarks you make without malice. What you say and do can erode your employees' spirit and contribute to all manner of performance problems.

In these pages, we make it possible for you to *see* the invisible spotlight, to *see the payoff* in being ever mindful of the impact you have on your management relationships. We show you how a conscious, considered approach to creating the foundation of these relationships is essential to your effectiveness and your employees' sense of satisfaction and success.

Our objective is to help you think about the management role and the pivotal moments you face in it. We hope the book makes you think as carefully and deeply as our consulting clients have over the past thirty-five years. We wrote it to create an opportunity for you to take stock of what you do, how you do it, and how you want to do it. Whether you're a brand new, first-line supervisor, an experienced middle manager, or a seasoned senior executive, you'll find something here worth your time and contemplation.

We don't burden you with esoteric, scholarly concepts. We don't fill your head with a litany of inspirational leadership quotes by corporate celebrities, sports heroes, or historical warriors. There aren't any to-do lists. You won't find clever management tips and tricks in the page margins.

Each of these approaches to presenting management ideas has its place. But all share the goal of reducing the practice of management to a formula. For understandable reasons, each strives to boil down a complex profession to a set of neat principles and prescriptions. Yet these can only get you through the simple, mechanical tasks of management. In truth, no paint-by-numbers approach can adequately prepare you for the ambiguities and nuances of the management role.

Instead we address the inconvenient, messy realities head on. Not with a recipe, but through stories and commentary.

If you think about it, your most profound and enduring lessons since childhood have been learned through stories, not how-to lists: from fairy tales to children's rhymes and parables that your parents read to you at bedtime; from religious fables to Tom Sawyer and Nancy Drew; from biographies and memoirs to poignant song lyrics and engrossing novels. Stories have inspired you to find life's morals and come to your own conclusions about them.

We think this is the kind of learning that sticks – realistic, vivid examples that respect your capacity to make sense of them and to tailor their lessons to your own circumstances.

The chapters distill into a collection of real-life scenarios our nearly four decades of management consultations in a wide variety of work settings. We've selected situations that illustrate the more common and compelling management moments our clients have faced. We're confident you'll recognize many of them. Each should act like a mirror, reflecting your own challenges in the invisible spotlight. Of course we add our own two cents along the way – our own observations and insights gained as "intimate outsiders" – in the hopes of enriching what you take from our experiences.

Read only one or two of these chapters in a sitting, even if you have time and enthusiasm to take on more. Let the ideas digest before you plow ahead. Otherwise the stories become an undifferentiated stream, and the finer points can get lost in the flow.

No doubt some of the ideas will make intuitive sense to you; they'll echo your own instincts and common sense. Others will challenge you to think differently; they are a new angle on the management role. Still others may make sense to you only down the road, with further reflection and experience. We'll consider any and all of these outcomes worth the effort we've put into this project.

To our clients who might be concerned that we have used your dilemmas in the unseen spotlight as examples of managerial wisdom and waywardness, let us assure you we have. You have been, after all, our teachers. But let us also assure you we've protected your identity while preserving your dignity and humanity.

Finally, a note on pronouns: Throughout the book, we've used the first-person singular rather than plural: "I" instead of "we." After much back and forth, we decided that this literary device would be clearer for our readers. In truth, we don't work with clients as a team; each client is served by one or the other of us. So representing the book's many scenarios as if both of us were at ringside would be awkward and inaccurate. Having made this first decision, the desire to avoid confusion compelled us to stay with the first-person singular as we shifted back and forth between story and commentary.

Accordingly, "I" hope this book persuades you that management is a consequential and honorable profession. As you'll see, getting the most from your employees depends on how you conduct yourself and your relationships in the invisible spotlight.

Craig Wasserman
Doug Katz

PART I:
THE MANAGEMENT
RELATIONSHIP

If you treat an individual... as if he were what he ought to be and could be, he will become what he ought to be and could be.

~Johann Wolfgang von Goethe

CHAPTER ONE:
HOW MUCH YOU MATTER

Underestimating your impact on employees' lives
is the single most common management mistake

Your employees talk about you every night at dinner. The meal is placed on the table and your employee's significant other asks the fateful question, "How was work today, dear?" The next words are about you. Sometimes directly, sometimes indirectly. Either way, they're about you.

"It was great today; my boss was out at a conference." Or "It was really aggravating; the boss was at an all-day meeting and left no one in charge." Or "It was aggravating; she was training and left Larry in charge." Or "Excellent day. I finished my project ahead of schedule, and my boss was all over me with gratitude."

When you come, where you go, and what you do in between are of the utmost importance to your employees. They've been conditioned since childhood to please authority: parents, teachers, clergy, coaches, police officers…and now their manager.

Yet the most frequent and fundamental mistake managers like you make is to underestimate their impact. Managers invariably fail to recognize the influence they exert over their employees' lives – personal as much as professional. They fail to recognize how much they matter.

More often than not, you're on automatic pilot. Your instincts are in control. You don't consciously choreograph your impact. And because you're not consistently mindful of the influence you have, you're prone to overlook, underestimate, and misuse your power.

THE POWER OF MOMENTS

So much of your relationship with employees is forged in brief, unscripted moments. Sometimes the moments are dramatic, sometimes quiet and fleeting. A passing conversation with an employee, a glance of approval or disapproval, a gesture of encouragement when an employee's confidence flags – these are the moments that can make or break your relationship with anyone who works for you.

Unfortunately, the popular management literature of the day encourages you to develop "reliable management systems" and a "consistent management style" as if the secret to success were in your everyday, predictable management routines. The fugitive moments I'm referring to here barely get a mention. Let me assure you that you can raise or lower the spirits of an employee, eliminate or perpetuate confusion, make important things happen or stall…all in a matter of seconds. And yet you might barely notice what you've done.

Once you pay attention though, you can create these pivotal moments rather than relying on your reflexes. The trick is to consciously control the influence you have, to act with intention. This control – this self-control really – makes it possible to turn a glancing moment into a lasting result. *These moments form the foundation of the management relationship.*

The violinist can't make music without first tuning her strings. The golfer can't sink a putt without first setting his hands in a proper grip. The actor can't captivate her audience without learning her lines. And the manager can't inspire his staff to deliver and innovate to their potential without cultivating a professional relationship.

If you're in a management role – whether out of desire or duty or fate – you must understand that at the core of your work are your management relationships. No amount of inspired business savvy, motivational energy, administrative skill, marketing expertise, or technological genius will compensate for an unhealthy relationship. None of these talents will bear the best possible fruit unless your management relationship is well watered.

THE BURDEN OF THE RELATIONSHIP

Think about the balance of responsibility in a healthy manager-employee relationship. Would you say it's 50/50, each of you contributing equally to the relationship's success? How about 60/40, with one or the other assuming a greater load?

Too many managers, new and seasoned, step into their role assuming the relationship is a 50/50 affair, and this begins their slide into ineffectiveness. Their problem is that they want to apply the ideals of equality and shared responsibility. But while these ideals are vital to the longevity of most relationships, they just don't apply to the professional management of employees. The management relationship is not like most others. It's unique because of the obligations that accompany it and the fact that it exists within an organizational hierarchy.

In this unusual relationship, the responsibility for creating a durable foundation isn't 50/50, and that's because the balance of power isn't 50/50. It isn't a marriage. It isn't a friendship. You and your employees aren't siblings, classmates, or business partners. In fact, despite what some management gurus would have you believe, you're not even teammates.

In this unusual relationship, you shoulder a disproportionate burden for the foundation. To say you shoulder as much as 80% would not be an overstatement.

And guess what: *your employees don't want it to be any different.* No matter how it may seem, no matter how you may want it, your employees don't want your friendship. They want your leadership.

You can try to avoid this by acting like an equal, and it might even change things on the surface. But it won't change the balance of responsibility. Nor will it change what your employees want and expect from you. No matter how hard you work at egalitarianism, the responsibility for what happens within the relationship and how it happens falls to you first. Think 80/20.

THE MANAGEMENT RELATIONSHIP

Mind you, we're talking here about the success or failure of the management *relationship*, not the performance of employees or of the organization. Our subject isn't the achievement of individual performance goals or corporate goals.

Instead, we're concerned with the *foundation* that underlies and enables the achievement of goals. We're talking about the alliance you create with employees, no matter whether their temperaments and skills are optimal for the job, and no matter whether broader institutional, economic, and marketplace conditions are favorable or grim.

This book concentrates on your ability to preserve a basic level of respect, confidence, and goodwill between your employees and yourself – whether their performance is good or bad; whether you're taking a popular or unpopular action; whether you're welcoming an employee on his first day of work or escorting him out the door on his last day.

I was not destined to be a great basketball player. Certainly not compared to the bigger, stronger, naturally gifted kids I played with at our community center. My junior high school coach made sure I knew it. He was chronically disparaging, scornful when I made mistakes in practice, and "forgetful" that I was on the bench each game, eager to play. He gave me no advice on how to get better. He'd decided I couldn't get better.

I tried out for the high school team anyway. I made the cut. The high school coach included me in every drill. He pushed me to do better, always with just the right amount of pressure. He encouraged me to try new moves more suited to my body type and athletic disposition. He also pulled no punches about my chances of playing in college. He knew they were remote, and he told me so. But he never humiliated me. He just wanted me to be realistic about my future. He was honoring his commitment to honesty with his players.

Neither of these coaches was responsible for my athletic limitations. But the first created a hurtful, adversarial relationship. His indifference drew far less out of me than I had to offer. My high school coach cultivated an alliance. He got everything I had to give.

Both coaches were in control of the coach/player relationship. Their control was rooted in their authority...the same kind of authority that a parent, teacher, or manager wields. People in these positions are *architects*. They shoulder the burden of creating the conditions that will maximize the potential of those in their care.

LOOKING IN ALL THE WRONG PLACES

Have you ever noticed how many hundreds of books are written about being an effective manager and how few are written about being an effective employee? Just do a quick scan of Amazon's pages or the shelves of your neighborhood bookstore. They're stocked high with the management secrets of Attila the Hun, Machiavelli, Abraham Lincoln, or your favorite winning athletic coach, business executive, political figure, or management consultant. You can read about how to be a one-minute manager, how to lead a high-performing team, how to use consensus management, how to imbue your management style with Zen. You can survey thousands of management styles and tricks. You can learn what academic researchers and consulting firms have discovered about management success.

But you won't find a lot of books about how to be a successful employee. That's because how-to books for employees don't have much value.

I learned why when I was starting my career. A client asked me to run a training program called "How to Manage your Supervisor." I was inexperienced and idealistic. I was also hungry for work. Mostly, I believed in the power of candid, rational communication to offset the damage when management relationships go south.

So I developed the program. The results were abysmal.

The moment the participants began describing their trials and anxieties with inept, unthinking, ornery supervisors, I saw I had the wrong people in the classroom. The managers needed the training, not their employees. The managers were in a position to solve these operational problems and communication ruptures, not their employees.

The only successful aspect of the entire program was the attendance; they were turning people away at the door. It confirmed every suspicion I had that managers exert a powerful influence on their employees and yet are unaware of its extent. Managers are either preoccupied with their own needs and anxieties, or they're depending on their reflexes and "natural style" rather than a deliberate approach to their obligations. They are simply oblivious to how much they matter.

An employee doesn't set the tone, standards, or direction for the way the two of you work. The foundation of this relationship always falls to you. You're the *architect*. You're the one responsible to create the conditions that promote your employees best work. It all boils down to an inescapable truth, a truth at the core of this entire book.

If the foundation of the management relationship is solid, it's because you're doing something right. If the foundation falters or fails, it's because you're doing something wrong. It's that simple and that difficult.

Being natural is simply a pose.

~Oscar Wilde

CHAPTER TWO:
THE INVISIBLE SPOTLIGHT

Management is a role performed in an unseen spotlight;
you have to write your script with care and calculation

C. S. Forester wrote a delightful series of books about Horatio Hornblower. The series recounts the fictional character's lifelong adventures in the British navy during the time of Napoleon. Forester takes us through the full breadth of Hornblower's career, from midshipman through commander and captain to admiral of the fleet. All in all, they are riveting tales of seamanship, heroism, and leadership.

Over the course of the series, the Hornblower character matures into a revered and beloved leader: wise, daring, controlled, and deeply human. Ironically, he was cursed by seasickness all his life. In the first days of every tour of sea duty, this quintessential seafarer had to endure a miserable period of queasy acclimation to the relentless rocking and swaying of his ship. Of course, this adjustment period coincided with one of Hornblower's precedent-setting management challenges. The first days were when he would be making his initial impressions on the crew. His behavior during this period would establish how his men would regard him and how business would be conducted.

We find our hero spending hours in his cabin as his ships set sail, struggling in private to soothe a stomach turned upside down by the vessel's bobs and weaves. But Hornblower the manager knows the needs of his seamen. He knows all too well how important it is for them to see and hear and interact with their new captain. His men need to take a measure of him; to decide how it will be to serve under him; to learn what he values and what he is indifferent to; to assess if they can follow him when their lives are on the line. So every two hours, he wraps his retching body in uniform and walks the deck, chatting with the watch crew and "being seen."

Despite his compromised – and embarrassing – physical condition, Hornblower would show himself to be in control. His rounds and conversations were orchestrated to make an impression. His impact was *designed*. The captain was keenly aware of the moments he was creating, down to the slightest details. He knew that, as a leader, he was in an invisible spotlight.

I was fascinated as a young boy by Forester's books. Hornblower's reflections on self-control won my respect. He was my first model of a leader, mindful of his role and wholehearted in his commitment to enact it purposefully.

A SWEEPING CHANGE

Of course, purposeful management is not the stuff of fiction alone. I've seen the same inspired leadership in real life.

Several years ago, I was helping a community fire department establish salary parity across its neighboring fire houses. In the course of that work, I had the opportunity to watch the progression of a young officer to the senior ranks. Fire services are paramilitary organizations; their promotional procedures are rigorous. This young officer had applied to fill an open position for lieutenant. He and the other aspirants took the various tests and underwent a grueling trial of assessment exercises and individual and panel interviews. At the end of the six-week process, during the weekly station meeting, it was announced that he had been awarded the promotion. Hearty and heartfelt pats on the back followed from co-workers, superiors, and even fellow applicants.

The next morning I was back at the station for the final meeting of my consulting engagement. I took a prolonged lap around the garage, walking among the fire trucks. On many previous visits I would seek out the firefighters, emergency medical technicians, and vehicle maintenance mechanics, barraging them with questions about their assignments and their vehicles, indulging my childhood fascination with the life of a fireman. But what caught my attention on this last morning was the newly appointed lieutenant. He was busily sweeping the floors. I remember distinctly that the announcement the day before made his promotion effective immediately. Yet he was sweeping.

After my meeting I sought the lieutenant out. He was in his new office reviewing paperwork. I asked him how it felt to be the lieutenant. He told me he was excited, honored by the opportunity, and eager to meet the challenge. He was quick to add that he still had much to learn.

I mentioned I'd seen him sweeping earlier and wondered if that was part of a lieutenant's job description. He chuckled, "Duty rosters are for a week. I began the week with the assignment, and there's no excuse not to finish it. I also want these guys to see that nothing I ever ask of them is beneath me." After a pause he added, "You know they're watching me now." I nodded. Like Hornblower, he knew he was in an unseen spotlight. He wasn't finishing his week's assignment out of duty alone. He was sweeping for all to see. He was creating a purposeful moment crafted to communicate a distinct leadership message.

OFFICE POLITICS

A new vice president joined a large company to which I was consulting. A vacant corner office was assigned to him and was scheduled for repainting in advance of his start date. But a miscommunication between the Facilities Department and the contractor delayed the job by a few weeks.

When he arrived for his first day, there was some confusion about where he should park himself. His staff wanted to impress him with their helpfulness. Some offered their own offices; others suggested comparable corner space on other floors. But the VP noticed an unoccupied office on his department's floor and insisted that he set up there for the interim. The office was sterile and cramped, with barely enough space for a visitor's chair. The view from the small window behind the desk was of the pigeon-decorated cooling towers on the roof next door. There was no nearby area in the hall to seat an assistant.

Not an office befitting a corporate officer. Yet the VP insisted. He used that office for two weeks as his home base. He met his staff and colleagues there and spent hours at the desk, acquainting himself with the organization he'd just joined.

When I stopped in to meet him some days later, he made no reference to his undersized quarters; never reached for a polished explanation nor an assurance that soon he would move to a more suitable space. He allowed his decision to speak for itself. He knew his behavior was making a statement about his values and his leadership. He knew those around him were noticing and hearing through the grapevine about his choices. He was yet another manager who understood that his people were talking about him at dinner – that he was front and center in an invisible spotlight.

He made a deliberate decision. He regarded the logistical delay not as an inconvenience but as an opportunity rich with symbolism.

HIDE AND SEEK

Hornblower, the fire service lieutenant, and the corporate VP recognized the possibilities and obligations inherent in the precedent-setting days of a new management position. But these aren't the only moments in which engineered actions distinguish the superior leader from the pack.

I was shooting the breeze with a research institute president's secretary one morning (one never knows when one might need so well-placed a person to open a door or say a good word). After some chitchat she asked, "Why don't you go in to see him? He's available." His door was closed, and I had just assumed he was out and about. "Just knock," she encouraged.

I did just that and opened the door a few inches. Sure enough, there he was at his desk, reading the morning paper. He signaled me to come in and close the door behind me as he folded his newspaper and laid it to the side. I was surprised to see him not up to his neck in something of great import and asked him flat out what in the world he was doing.

"I'm hiding."

He read my bemused expression and explained, "My folks are preparing their presentations for me on the new overseas project we're launching. Every bone in my body wants to march out there, drop in on their meetings, and see where they are. But there's no doubt in my mind that if I did, I'd make a pain in the ass of myself, forcing them to focus on me rather than on this initiative. And I'd probably not be able to help myself from getting involved. They're smart people. I want their ideas, not a regurgitated version of my own. So here I hide."

With a sigh, he finished his thought. "Now I have you to talk with until 11:30, lunch until 1:00, a meeting with a science advisory board at 2:00, and then a progress review for the remainder of the day with a department uninvolved in this initiative…firewalls that should keep me from doing any damage until tomorrow when we look at the project as a team."

I was impressed. He knew his role, and he knew his impact. He knew he had to subjugate his impulse to take charge. As an employee over the years, he had been a star performer. He enjoyed countless accolades and a steady career rise. But now, as the president, he knew there were times when he had to be a supportive audience for the next generation of superstars.

Make no mistake: by making himself scarce, he did not elude the invisible spotlight! Quite the contrary. His absence was as conspicuous as his physical presence would have been. It illustrates both the opportunity and the rub for a manager: you can close your door, you can silence yourself, you can leave the building, but you can't step out of the invisible spotlight.

CHOOSING TO BE BORED

In another instance, I was attending a two-day environmental health and safety retreat for a large industrial corporation. Some four hundred health and safety officers were in attendance. Though sessions like these are indispensable to the success of corporate enterprises, this one was sure to be a long, tedious affair.

The meeting began traditionally enough with the EH&S vice president providing an overview of the two days and reviewing the company's year-to-date results. The chief executive officer then took the podium. She addressed the role of the EH&S organization in safeguarding the company's reputation as a good neighbor, a law-abiding company, and a profitable business. At the CEO's request, I then spoke about the importance of working smart with each other and with the sometimes-resistant operating units of the company that this crowd trained and monitored.

When I finished, a break was called, and fifteen minutes later the throng returned for the second morning session. My seat was next to the CEO's which I assumed would be vacant. In large gatherings like this, my experience is that senior executives leave after playing their ceremonial parts. Much to my surprise, this CEO returned. After lunch, I was surprised again when she reappeared beside me.

By midafternoon, the meeting took the familiar turn that all such sessions take. The speeches droned, the eyes got heavy, the PowerPoints all began to look the same. It was like drinking a tall glass of sand. Necessary yes, but invigorating, not so much. Nonetheless, there the CEO sat, neither text messaging under the table nor doodling mindlessly on her pad.

By the afternoon break, my curiosity got the best of me. "What are you still doing here?" I asked. "You could have escaped long ago."

"You know, just about every day I talk about the importance of what these folks do," she said. "What message would it send if I left? These people are watching me. They want to know if I mean what I say – if I actually believe their work is vital or just give speeches about how vital it is. Look, there's no question I'm bored to tears, but I'm here for the rest of today and much of tomorrow."

I loved this woman's perspective. She refused to use her status to cut corners. She was working hard to camouflage her boredom. She would not risk an impression of duplicity. But most important, she understood that her impact was being made not just at the podium in the real spotlight, but while sitting at her assigned seat in the unseen one.

As a result, four hundred people were assured that their roles were relevant and critical. There is no doubt in my mind they were thinking the same thing I was: I can't believe she's still here!

It's often said that small minds talk about people; large minds talk about ideas. Well, when it comes to our leaders, we all have small minds. We all talk about them. We all watch them. The great ones know it. They manage the impressions they make with a purpose. They know how much a manager matters.

MANAGEMENT IS WORK

This concept of the invisible spotlight was never made clearer to me than by Bruce, the area director of a large pharmaceutical company.

Bruce had asked me to help him think through the strategy, events, and main topics for his annual managers' meeting in Atlantic City. Over several days and dozens of hours, we worked out a lively, informative, upbeat agenda. After all, it had been an outstanding year for his area, and he wanted the three-day meeting to recognize this in a meaningful way and provide some inspiration and direction for the year ahead.

As we put the final touches on his plans and rose from the conference table, I encouraged him to "enjoy your meeting. It should be a great time." But Bruce didn't respond immediately or gratuitously. Clearly he was thinking about the three days before him.

"This isn't going to be much fun for me. I have work to do. I have names to remember, people to recognize. Husbands and wives to meet for the first time who will feel pressure not to say the wrong thing in front of me. Comments that need to be well placed. I've got to be on my game for the next seventy-two hours. Lots of moments to manage. This will be work."

He could have added, "I'll be under a spotlight. They'll all be watching."

If you have a job without aggravation,
you don't have a job.

~Malcolm Forbes

CHAPTER THREE: MANAGEMENT IS WORK

Managing involves unnatural, uncomfortable behavior; the role takes practice, self-reflection, and discipline

A trucking company's vice president of operations asked me to spend a day on site with Phil, his district manager in Cleveland. Phil was a big man, six foot six, 260 pounds, who managed over two hundred employees for his company. His presence and manner were imposing to say the least. When I first met him, I remember thinking he could snap me in two at the slightest provocation.

Phil was wrapping up his first year at the helm in Cleveland. By any number of business measures – revenue, sales, expense control, safety, process improvements, record keeping, turnover – Phil's first year was a stunning success. But the operations VP had detected a few murmurs about Phil's "management style" during his own trips to the district. Because Phil was so promising, the VP wanted to nip any stylistic problems in the bud.

As was my routine with a new client, I spent an hour with Phil before meeting anyone else. We had coffee in his office and exchanged histories. He was neither certain why I had made this visit nor particularly comfortable with my role – pretty typical of first consulting encounters with managers whose superiors have made all the arrangements. Nonetheless, Phil's approach wasn't cautious. Without embellishment, he came right out and asked, "What are you here for?"

"Phil, I'm a management consultant. My expertise is in assessing how you use your management authority to oversee your district. To the extent you want my assistance, I can help you perform your management role as effectively as possible. My job is to hold up a mirror that reflects the impact you're having on your organization and to show you where you can make improvements. So I'll take a snapshot today. I'll speak with your department heads and some of their subordinates. I'll watch your organization in action. I'll form some impressions and make some assessments. I'll share them with you at the end of the day along with my best advice. Then I'll be on my way. If what I have to say is helpful, we both benefit. You can contact me if additional counsel would be of use. If my advice is not helpful, we'll shake hands and wish each other well."

The reality was that Phil had no say in the job I was going to do. His VP had sent me to evaluate his impact on the morale of his organization.

Faced with no alternative, Phil grudgingly accepted my presence. He laid out a schedule of meetings for me with his department heads and built in time for whomever else I might bump into as I meandered through the district's accounting and sales offices, vehicle and equipment yards, dispatch office, and repair shop.

Our morning conversation had broken the ice, and throughout the day we exchanged pleasantries as we passed each other in the busy halls, garages, and service bays. The passing exchanges left the impression with those employees who observed them that Phil and I were on more familiar terms than we were. This was by design.

I had told Phil his employees would be as eager as he to know why I was in the district. To minimize uncertainty and discomfort, I was going to tell those I interviewed that Phil himself had invited me when he learned that headquarters was making my services available to *all* district managers. In other words, I would say that Phil was seeking the snapshot, not the higher-ups. This went down particularly well with him. We'd just met. He was suspicious and for good reason. But at least he saw I had no intention of humiliating him.

THE CONSULTANT'S MIRROR

At four o'clock, after a day of formal interviews, casual conversations, and many observations, Phil and I reconvened in his office for our debriefing. This man oozed a "direct-and-to-the-point" attitude from our first encounter that morning, so I wasted no time summarizing what I had learned.

In his year as district manager, the organization had made great strides. He had brought order and discipline to Cleveland. The stiff standards of excellence he had introduced, though initially protested by his employees, were now a point of obvious and genuine pride.

It was apparent to those with whom I spoke that Phil had brought significant improvements to the business. Its profitability was testament as was the praise of his staff: "Phil turned us around." "Before Phil, we were dysfunctional, marching without a beat, pure and simple." "Phil is sharp, straightforward, committed, and gets things done." "He's a no-nonsense guy; he knew what he wanted from us. And we've delivered. Just as important, we've learned a helluva lot about trucking, about organization, and about pushing beyond our limits."

But one other theme ran through every conversation I had with his supervisors and staff. It was, of course, what brought me to Cleveland in the first place. Phil scared the crap out of everyone. Apparently, he made *everyone* think he was capable of snapping them in two at the slightest provocation.

After I presented his achievements as seen through the eyes of his staff, I moved the conversation to Phil's management style. I'd be lying if I said it wasn't with some trepidation.

I explained that in his enthusiasm to turn the organization around, he'd taken no prisoners. Just about everyone told some version of the same story: a supervisor demeaned in midsentence for a scheduling procedure that Phil thought was misguided; a newer supervisor's safety improvement recommendation harshly dismissed because Phil declared it too costly for the presumed benefits; a department head's carefully conceived plans for the layout of the truck bays summarily overridden. The word in the hallways was that Phil had no patience, his ideas were the only viable ones, he was callous, thoughtless, intimidating. He was like the cow that gives good milk but then knocks the bucket over.

Working in Phil's world was hard on his workforce. It was beyond just stretching to do their level best as professionals. It had become personal. The relentless pressure had become demoralizing. Each supervisor described the same journey: from initial skepticism soon after Phil arrived, to full throttle enthusiasm and an eagerness to please, to a sense of tentativeness and cowering – both at work and after hours – as the atmosphere became abusive. Several supervisors were actively seeking other jobs. Not surprisingly, these were some of Phil's best and most promising.

THE RISK OF SELF-ACCEPTANCE

This should have been a pretty tough message for Phil to digest. But as I held up the proverbial mirror, Phil simply looked at me, occasionally nodding in agreement. When I was finished, he reflected a moment. Then, "You're not telling me anything I don't already know. My family has been telling me these things for years. I don't suffer fools well. That's just the way I am."

I had to respect the guy for his candor. He could never be accused of dipping his words in sugar.

But his self-acceptance was self-destructive. "Phil, we've just come to the reason your VP sent me here. He didn't give you this job so you could be the way you 'am.' He didn't give you this job so you could be a bastard. He gave it to you with the expectation that you would be a professional leader. Those are far from the same thing."

Phil sat calmly and considered my response. So I continued, "If you want to be a barbarian with your family and friends, there's nothing I can do about it. Nor would I want to. For all I know, they love you the way you are; if they do, you're a fortunate guy. But at this company, working as a manager, you're expected to work at *being* a manager. You can't simply rely on your 'natural ways.' You're the guy responsible for making these workplace relationships work, not driving them into the turf. You're the guy who has to develop these supervisors into confident captains, not shadows of themselves, limping away for safe harbor. You're the guy who has to establish an atmosphere that encourages best efforts, not one that exposes vulnerabilities and insecurities. Being an effective manager is your job. It's a set of skills that needs to be mastered. In this regard, you're failing."

No doubt in my mind, at that moment Phil wanted to dismiss me as he had his own staff too many times. To his credit, he didn't take a single swipe. Not then, nor in the months following as we worked together *at his request* on his approach to management.

As the months wore on, looking together at example after example of the moments Phil was creating, he slowly (and often reluctantly) realized that his delivery was as important as what he delivered. The means of transportation had as much impact as the cargo. He gradually accepted that his superiors hadn't ordered him to succeed by any means necessary. Yes, there was a cleanup to be done, but there was also the long-term health of the organization and its people to cultivate.

He slowly accepted these things because: (1) he knew his superiors were concerned about his approach (I wouldn't have been sent to Cleveland otherwise); (2) his employees had now expressed their frustration out loud; (3) he knew the mirror I'd held up was accurate – and I eventually persuaded him that I'd held it up to help him; and (4) practical alternatives to his approach were beginning to make sense to him – more thoughtful and productive ways of handling his interactions were showing signs of paying off. Mostly, however, Phil came to accept how much his management approach mattered because he wanted to be successful.

Phil worked hard at catching himself. He began to allow others to succeed and err more on their own and to learn from both. He began to insist on the critical things, recognizing that not everything is critical. He learned that his natural impatience was a virtue so long as it served to energize, not humiliate. And most important for Phil, he came to appreciate that his employees wanted to please him; he needed to master the art of making that possible for them.

MANAGEMENT IS WORK

Phil is every manager. In a broad sense, his puzzle is your puzzle: how to piece together your personal virtues and flaws with the job of leading. The first pieces come together only when you stop assuming that the fit will be natural or that "how you are" is how you can and should manage. Every manager has to hone the virtues that strengthen his or her managerial relationships and find a place to shelve the ones that do damage.

We've all known managers who are overbearing, glib, emotionally volatile, tightly wound, scattered, over-intellectual, exhaustingly perfectionistic, intolerant of criticism, or fearful of hurting anyone's feelings. The litany of ill-fitting and missing qualities that managers inflict on employees is endless. But none of these managers is a freak of nature. With rare exception, they are good people. They are you.

Management is hard work. It requires many organizational skills and many relationship skills. *Why would anyone expect to have them in their arsenal "naturally"?* Those who persevere do, over time, perform more effectively. It's worth pointing out, by the way, that these managers don't necessarily change as people. They don't automatically become better parents or spouses or friends or neighbors. They become better managers. They perform more intelligently in their management role during their working hours. They develop a keener appreciation for their obligations and challenges in the unseen spotlight.

Your work involves unnatural, uncomfortable behavior that may not feel like the "real you." If you long to express the real you – to give free rein to your instincts – go on vacation. Work takes practice, self-reflection, and discipline.

PART II:
MANAGEMENT MOMENTS

In giving advice, seek to help,
not please, your friend.

~Solon

CHAPTER FOUR:
MOMENTS OF DISCOMFORT

People don't change when they're comfortable;
they change when they're uncomfortable

Margaret was the executive vice president for west coast operations and Alan managed one of her statewide marketing teams. One Friday afternoon, Margaret called Alan into her office to promote him to director of west coast marketing. Alan was thrilled. He had suspected for some time that the position would be his in the future, but the future came sooner than he'd imagined. The two discussed the region's business opportunities for an hour or so, and Margaret gave Alan a copy of the promotion announcement that was going out that afternoon. They shook hands and wished each other a good weekend.

The two met again at 8:40 the following Monday morning, moving aside for each other as they passed in opposite directions through the front door. Margaret was leaving for a meeting downtown, and Alan was arriving to start his first week as director. Still buoyant about his good fortune, Alan greeted Margaret with a hearty, "Good morning!" Margaret responded with a firm, "Work starts at 8:00." Alan, caught off guard by her terseness, spurted, "Oh, I was in Sacramento this weekend and woke at 5:00 to get here on time, but traffic was heavier than I had anticipated...." Margaret wasn't listening as she briskly walked on. Alan headed for his office, unsettled.

I know the exchange seared both parties, because they talked about it with me several times over the years when I consulted to their organization.

From Alan's vantage point: "Here it was my first day as director, and she pings me before I'm even in the building. I knew she was a stickler for punctuality, and I let her down. I felt like crap."

Margaret didn't fare much better in the aftermath: "If I had one concern about promoting Alan, it was that he would live too large as a director. I knew I'd have to watch his expense reports and adherence to company protocol; I'd have to call him quickly on extravagances. Little did I know it would be required on his first day, literally as he was taking his first steps into the new job. I felt like crap."

To me, this episode is poetry. It underscores that moments of discomfort are unavoidable in a healthy relationship between committed professionals. In fact, healthy relationships remain healthy *because* leaders don't shy away from these episodes. They use them to assure that their expectations and observations are unambiguous. Any immediate anxiety is offset by the longer-term value of forthrightness.

Good managers confront issues when they're small, speak the words that must be spoken despite the unavoidable sting, and recognize that jangled nerves will repair themselves over time if the exchange is intended to help, not humiliate an individual.

For the moment, pass no judgment on Margaret's concern for timeliness. Put aside whether it's important to you or not and simply accept that, in her position, it's her legitimate prerogative to value punctuality. Now just imagine what would have happened had Margaret not expressed her displeasure. Alan would have gone through the day oblivious that his late arrival had disturbed his boss. Or maybe he would have concluded that seniority has its privileges, confirmed in part by his boss's silence about his transgression.

Margaret would have gotten to her car in a slow burn. "That guy has nerve. I promote him on Friday and he cuts up on Monday." She might have begun to second-guess her decision; maybe even consider if the promotion could be withdrawn. Or maybe use the drive downtown to concoct any number of indirect ways to convey her displeasure. Later that day, she might edgily say something out of context to Alan just to discharge her pent up irritation. Alan would flinch at the jab without grasping the meaning or motive. And knowing Margaret, she would feel guilty about her awkward, unwarranted retaliation.

But this is a success story. Margaret did express her displeasure. She spoke directly. She addressed the infraction immediately; headed it off before her frustration mounted. Both parties were uncomfortable. But both weathered the turbulence. Margaret came to realize that, in that moment, she was establishing an organizational precedent – a precedent of sufficient importance to counterbalance the ruffled feathers. She was seasoned enough to know that upbeat, affirming conversations with her employees are necessary to make a relationship successful but not sufficient.

Alan came to realize that he was now working for a professional who would say what she meant and mean what she said – a lesson that had a profound effect on their relationship and on the way Alan would mature as a manager. The two worked successfully with each other for years to come. Margaret spoke the words that needed to be spoken in that fateful, fugitive moment.

DISCOMFORT AND CHANGE

The idea that you can discuss unwanted news or provide a critical assessment and at the same time keep an employee smiling is silly. There's just no way around the fact that speaking the truth about a failure, an oversight, or an inconvenient development is thorny for all parties.

And yet, over the past half century, we've clung to the idea that managers should manage conflict without anyone feeling ill at ease. We ask managers to read books, watch instructional DVDs, and attend training classes on how to achieve a mutually satisfying, "win-win solution" through "open, empathic dialog" with their employees. We've somehow convinced ourselves that if only managers polish their communication skills, change can be comfortable.

Unfortunately, managers too often come away from these "lessons" believing they can discuss serious problems and deficiencies without causing any pain and suffering. How "comfortably" the conversation goes becomes their measure of success. But here's the thing: *Contrary to popular belief, people don't change and improve when they're comfortable. They change when they're uncomfortable.*

When managers varnish the truth, they may avoid tension and conflict, but they'll fix nothing. They'll improve nothing. And this is because they create no incentive, opportunity, or direction for change.

THE COMPASSION PARADOX

That's what tripped up Peter, a particularly kindly manager. Peter believed he had to coat bad news to help employees swallow it. It's by far one of the most common missteps I see.

After a period of observation and mentoring, Peter concluded that one of his employees, Brent, was ill suited to the technical work of his department. Brent had some wonderful attributes, but a technical, analytical mind was not one of them.

With his boss's encouragement, Peter worked with a fellow manager to have Brent transferred to another, less detail oriented department. He then met with Brent in the hope of securing his consent. As I mentioned, Peter was a warmhearted gentleman and didn't want to foist the transfer on Brent. He believed a sincere and supportive conversation would bring Brent to acknowledge his own deficiencies and see the wisdom of the reassignment. Peter wanted a meeting of the minds…a happy ending.

Their conversation was civil, compassionate, and comfortable. But thoroughly unproductive. To Peter's surprise, Brent thought he was doing just fine in the department, learning and contributing more and more with every passing day. He appreciated that Peter was offering an alternative but respectfully declined, insisting he enjoyed his present position far too much. Peter was completely unprepared to respond to Brent's obvious misperceptions. He feared that challenging them would lower Brent's self-esteem. All Peter could think to do was repeat again and again how valuable Brent would be in the other department. Eventually and half-heartedly, Brent agreed to "think about it." It was the only concession Peter could get. The conversation that was supposed to make everyone happy ended in a state of muddy inconclusiveness.

Peter was benevolent but impotent. The premium he placed on cordiality obscured the message he needed to convey. The worst part was that Peter's "compassion" amounted to a grave disservice to Brent and to the organization. By creating the illusion of a choice, Peter misled Brent. In his attempt to spare Brent's feelings, Peter created complications and confusions that delayed the transfer. It also frayed Brent's nerves and his own and caused his superior to question his effectiveness as a manager.

Peter's boss asked me to meet with Peter to help get the matter back on track. Peter and I were no strangers to each other. Years earlier, he had been denied a promotion that he believed he deserved. The powers that be at the time considered him a strong candidate but believed he needed more seasoning. Peter was annoyed and hurt by the decision but hung in, worked hard, and kept his eyes open for a second chance.

Now in a management role, he was paddling too carefully, making no waves. He knew his handling of the conversation with Brent had gone wrong, and he'd done some thinking about it. He explained to me that his "negotiations" with Brent had convinced him more than ever of the wisdom of a transfer. He knew it was up to him to make it happen but couldn't envision the best way to persuade Brent.

I asked him if he remembered how he felt years ago when his promotion was denied. He smiled sheepishly. "I felt horrible." I asked him how he got over it. "I moped for a while and then I just sucked it up and applied myself."

"Did it turn out all right? Are you happy with where you are today?"

"Well until this, very much so!"

The point was made for both of us: Time is a great healer. Brent too would survive. I said, "Suck it up and do your job then! This isn't a negotiation. It's a management decision. And one you say you're convinced is the right one. If you mean it, then be respectful of Brent. Let him know the decision has been made." Peter was taken aback by my directness, but that's what the moment called for.

Ultimately, Peter made a specific plan for his next conversation with Brent. He formulated the words that would get his points across simply and unmistakably. He knew there might be some uneasiness, but he also knew the transfer was in all parties' best interests. He told Brent directly that he was being transferred and in all respects handled the situation with evenhandedness and respect.

Watch deliberate managers handle difficult conversations. Their objective is to speak clearly and frankly enough to *carve a path to change while protecting the relationship.* That is what Margaret did in a flash. That is what Peter didn't do in his first several hours of belabored conversation. *The truth is, some degree of discomfort sets the stage for change. The trick is not to avoid it but to manage it head on and with respect.*

Speak clearly, if you speak at all; carve every word before you let it fall.

~ Oliver Wendell Holmes

CHAPTER FIVE:
THE INTERNAL DIALOG

You can't rely on your reflexes alone when you need to walk a tight rope; managing important moments requires anticipation and rehearsal

To the untrained eye, it may appear that capable managers are endowed with a knack for thinking on their feet. They seem to know just what to say, just how to act. What's uncanny is how spontaneous their reactions seem. Unscripted. Off the cuff. Capable managers seem to respond in the moment, to the moment, without time or need for planning.

Don't be fooled.

Sure, all of us have had the good fortune of a sudden insight in the midst of turbulence. But managers with staying power don't count on their reflexes alone when they walk a tight rope. Nor do they expect the tightrope itself to somehow reveal how to balance on it.

Being *naturally* quick on your feet is a management myth. Quickness requires years of practice, lots of mistakes and recoveries, and careful preparation. The reality is that conscientious managers spend hours anticipating the rough roads they expect to travel. They score their important interactions the way a composer scores a symphony. I call this the *internal dialog*.

When managers prepare for pivotal conversations with their employees, they don't do it with a broad brush. In fact, what they do resembles the vivid, private rehearsals of a stage actor, or the pre-visualizations of an Olympic athlete. They don't imagine their challenges in general terms; they engineer them down to the particulars.

You've seen these managers as you commute to work. They're talking to themselves in their cars. Sometimes they'll turn their rear view mirrors toward themselves so they can speak into their own eyes. You see their lips moving, but they're not singing with the radio or having a Bluetooth chat. They're talking out loud to themselves. What you're catching a glimpse of are diligent managers in an internal dialog – anticipating how they'll navigate the ebbs and flows of a tough conversation with an employee.

ENVISIONING THE DETAILS

Trudy had to talk about a troubling development with one of her employees. Over a period of months, Barb had been late with several high-profile, time-sensitive assignments. At first, Trudy relied on gentle, roundabout comments and facial expressions to convey her disappointment to Barb. But these made no dent. Trudy even tried a sarcastic remark or two, but Barb just laughed them off, apparently oblivious to the intended message.

Inevitably, Trudy became aggravated. Barb was late with a critical field report, which complicated the schedules of other staff and threatened the delivery of a major departmental project.

It's not uncommon for managers to let issues like this play themselves out until disaster strikes. Many managers need their backs against a wall before they'll face the discomfort of a confrontation. The Manager's Prayer – "Maybe it will go away by itself" – is a common excuse for procrastinating. As good managers mature, they come to appreciate that catching performance issues early is a more productive and less disruptive alternative. More productive because it solves a problem before it gets out of hand; less disruptive in that it keeps drama in the management relationship at bay.

Trudy was a capable manager. More capable than her unfocused first stabs at the Barb problem would suggest. In fact, those far-too-casual early strategies illustrate what happens when a manager forgets that a healthy management relationship depends on a good deal of choreography.

Barb's late field report brought Trudy to her senses. So let's listen in on Trudy, driving her car to work on an overcast Tuesday morning, thinking about how best to approach her discussion with Barb:

> *I'll stop by her office this morning. No, I'll call her into mine. I want to be on my own turf. We'll sit at the table. I'll start by asking how things are going. Wait, that will open the door to digressions. This meeting isn't about how things are going. I need to confine the focus to missed deadlines.*

> *How should I begin? "Barb, why has it been difficult to get your work done on time these past few months? Did you know your last two assignments missed their deadlines?" Yes, that's specific. It establishes the subject and clearly implies the goal of the conversation. That's what I want.*

> *She'll say either, "No, I didn't realize they were late," or, "Yes, and that's because I need a new assistant, new computer, more time, more training...."*

> *Hmm. Then that's not the way to start. I don't want to hear either of those things. Come to think of it, it's not even her lateness that most concerns me! It's that Barb gives me no heads-up. That's more important than the missed deadline! Yeah, I want her to be on time, but giving me no clue when she's going to miss a*

date always delays everyone's work. It also sabotages the credibility of my commitments to my boss and colleagues. We look bad when we're late; we look worse when those affected don't know we're going to be!

I think I need to start this discussion with the facts. "Barb, your last two assignments were late, and I didn't learn about it until they were due and I came looking for them. It's become a pattern that really has to be fixed. There's just too much at stake." Then I'll wait. Let the silence fill the room.

What will she say? Possibly an excuse. "Well, on the first report I was waiting for James to finish his charts and graphs; on the second, it just required a lot more research and analysis than you and I planned for." That's when I'll have to put my stake in the ground. "Listen, there will always be reasons for missing a deadline, and I'll consider their legitimacy on a case by case basis. But the problem here is beyond the delays. The problem here is that you didn't inform me as soon as you knew."

Yes. That's the issue. No warning. A failure to keep me informed. That's what's disturbing me, and that's why we need to have this meeting. I've got to hit that point and stay with that point!

She may circle back to her excuse, "But James was holding me up!" I'll repeat the main point, "OK, and what prevented you from picking up the phone, walking into my office, sending me an e-mail to let me know?" Depending on how defensive she is, she might say, "I just didn't know James was going to take so long." And I won't budge. "But when it did become apparent that things were dragging out, you didn't raise a flag. And that's the recurring mistake!"

*Now. If I can get that central point to hit home, where
do I go from there? Knowing Barb, there will be some
emotionality. She's a proud person. She'll continue to
look for scapegoats and fail to accept her responsibility,
even if she sees no way to excuse her irresponsibility. I
have to make sure the conversation doesn't get personal;
I have to stay with her error in judgment and the simple
courtesy of advance notice. "Barb, when you let me
know ahead of time that you'll be late, I have options:
I can get you more resources, prepare my bosses for the
delay, change the scope of the assignment to fit the time
pressures. But when you keep me in the dark, I have
no recourse. And frankly, I lose confidence in your
dependability!"*

*Hmm. That'll be a hard blow for her to absorb. But
it has to be said. This is a lesson about professional
behavior, but it's also a lesson about my standards and
our relationship.*

*No matter how hard it is for Barb to swallow this,
I'll need to reinforce the message when we finish up
the conversation. How will I do that? "I want you
to see this conversation in context, Barb. Delays are
an unavoidable part of our business; we can live
with that reality. We have no choice but to live with
it. But without any warning, everyone's capacity to
adjust is restricted. It also compromises our working
relationship."*

Let's be clear: Trudy's internal conversation is an example of
exceptionally thorough and granular thinking. She very much
wanted to be effective with Barb, and she worked hard at it
on the drive to work. Most successful managers work through
"something like" this dialog. Usually the result isn't a complete
script but one or two key words and phrases that will make the

difference between a constructive interaction and a muddy one. Trudy's dialog represents a model to strive for.

Note how *vivid* her internal dialog is – the specificity of the words she chooses. She went to far greater lengths than simply putting the meeting on her calendar and hoping she'd figure out what to say when she got there. She wasn't going to rely on the tightrope to reveal how to balance on it.

Nor did she hope a few all-purpose, indefinite slogans would carry her through the conversation: "Be firm." "Make sure Barb knows who's boss." "Don't let Barb leave without understanding the problem." These are *impact* slogans; they define what *effect* you want to have in a situation, but they won't help you figure out *how to have* that effect.

Instead, Trudy constructed a detailed scenario which helped her see what was actually bothering her. She crafted her questions and statements in concrete language. She anticipated Barb's detours, defenses, and deceptions. She envisioned the transitions from point to point. She tested different strategies to see which would lead to dead ends and which would carve a path to change.

Put another way, Trudy forced herself through a full-blown dress rehearsal. She memorized her lines. She didn't hope for a favorable impact; she staged it. The precision of her internal dialog made it possible to master her own part in the drama. This, in turn, increased the chances that Barb would walk away with more than just frazzled nerves.

HOW AWKWARD CONVERSATIONS END

Psychotherapists are renowned for their fifty-minute hours. They'll rarely let a session with a patient go fifty-five minutes, never mind sixty-three. Despite common folklore, this is not a matter of nickel-and-diming patients (or at least not primarily).

It's actually based on the value of *brevity* and *economy* in emotional encounters.

When you have to manage prickly conversations like Trudy's with Barb, you'll find it challenging but worthwhile to keep them succinct. Not icy, not curt, not rushed, but businesslike. Bring them to a conclusion when it's apparent that your points have been understood.

Note I didn't say "end the meeting when your employee *agrees* with you." While your employee's agreement on a difficult issue obviously would be ideal, realistically these conversations often end with some degree of estrangement. It's OK. It doesn't mean the meeting failed. In fact, in many cases, it prefigures *success.* The uneasiness is a sign that the groundwork for change has been laid. What's important is that you've been *understood.*

Managers who get wound up in endless dialogs either have no idea how to finish up a conversation or they expect a consensus that can't be secured, at least not in one sitting. They're hoping (sometimes without realizing it) that the employee will stand, shake their hand, and say, "You know, I just didn't realize I was creating such a problem. I can guarantee you it will never happen again. From now on, whenever I'm falling behind schedule, you'll be the first to know. Thank you for bringing this to my attention. I so appreciate your candor and support!"

It's more likely that rocky conversations will end with the employee mumbling resentfully: "Can I leave now?" or "Is that it?" or "I'll just have to think about this" or even "Well, I guess we just don't see eye to eye on this."'When people are made to face an unflattering truth about themselves, they want to look away. It takes time for them to look back. Often it takes "alone" time. Time to rehash and reconsider. These are not feel-good conversations.

I learned this in a very personal way years ago. When we were newlyweds, my wife and I were on a long road trip together. She was working at a large law firm and began discussing a problem that was brewing between her and some of her colleagues.

Here I was with the woman I love, starting out our lives together. She was struggling with something right up my professional alley. I could really be helpful here, win some big points, maybe save the day. So I leaned into her story, soaked up all that she said, all that she implied, all that may have been going on that she wasn't aware of. I asked a few penetrating questions and reflected on the answers. Finally, I offered my blazingly astute observations and advice. I was eloquent and insightful. I know I was.

My new bride sat quietly in the passenger's seat. For twenty minutes, mile after mile, she sat in uninterrupted silence. This was a confusing reaction I had also experienced with some of my consulting clients. They'd outline a dilemma, we'd discuss it in detail, I'd offer my suggestions. Then silence. I never knew what to make of it. Had I said something offensive? Had I just been off-base? Was I boring them?

I endured my wife's silence until I thought I'd burst. Finally, I said, "Kath, you describe a problem to me, I offer my best counsel, and then…nada. What in the world are you thinking?" She seemed irritated by my intrusion. "You're right, OK? You're right about the situation. What you said is exactly what's going on in the office, it's how I've been mishandling it, and it's what I need to do going forward, OK? I'm thinking about it. OK?" So I backed off and left her with her thoughts.

I learned in that moment that when you speak a truth, especially when it's delicate or unflattering, it's best to let it bake in silence. Your work for the moment is done. The other person is the one who now has work to do. My wife needed some time alone. Your employees will need some time alone. Experienced managers are always on the lookout for clues that their work is done – that their employees are ready to rehash and reconsider in private. It's one of the things managers try to anticipate in their internal dialogs.

THE AFTERMATH

People don't accept their professional failings in a public pressure cooker. If they accept them at all, it's most often in personal moments – while sitting with a cup of coffee, mowing the lawn, taking a shower, falling off to sleep. At times like these, your employee will experience a wide range of reactions and insights. Like anger (*Who does she think she is?*); embarrassment (*Damn, she's figured me out*); fear (*My job's in real jeopardy now*); flight (*That's it, I've had it with this job; I'm outta here as soon as I can find something else*) and eventually – hopefully – resolve (*I will never let this happen again*).

Bruised sensibilities take time to heal no matter how much scripting and rehearsing you do in advance. The best you can do after a difficult encounter is provide some breathing room and otherwise engage in subtle acts of kindness and professionalism. In the days following a meeting like Trudy and Barb's, a purposeful manager will seek out the employee to give her an assignment, ask her opinion on a current issue, invite her to join a discussion…*in some way make contact to signal that the relationship need not be damaged.* The gesture is important; it communicates that criticism is as natural a part of the relationship as gratitude and appreciation. It lets the employee know that moments of discomfort are survivable and restorative.

The fundamental point is that preparation is so often the difference between a survivable, restorative encounter and a relationship-damaging confrontation. Take the time to anticipate how you'll navigate the potholes and dead ends of a delicate moment, and you'll begin to discover the invaluable opportunities that are hiding in them.

The fragrance always remains in the hand that gives the rose.

~Heda Bejar

CHAPTER SIX:
MOMENTS OF RECOGNITION

*More thought than you ever imagined goes into
the art of recognition and encouragement*

Moments of discomfort are an essential part of a healthy management relationship. But they're a means, not an end. For example, when Margaret told Alan that work starts at 8:00, her *objective* wasn't to make him uneasy; it was to reinforce an expectation. All such moments have a purpose beyond themselves. In the case of uncomfortable exchanges, that purpose is to open a door to the resolution of a problem or the realization of an employee's potential.

While moments of discomfort by their nature catch employees doing something wrong or unproductive, moments of recognition and encouragement catch employees when they're doing something right.

Many managers underestimate how much thought they need to put into the art of recognition and encouragement. Offering compliments is commonly considered the easy side of management, in stark contrast to discussing unpleasant realities. Nothing could be further from the truth. This side of the equation takes just as much practice and discipline.

To effectively recognize and encourage employees, you need to know what you're looking for. You need patience as the employee moves toward success in small, uneven steps. You need a sense of timing. And you need to use language that not only conveys that you're pleased but what you're pleased with. None of these skills comes naturally to most of us.

TIMING

I was visiting one of my clients' remote sites far from the home office where I met Ron, an employee whose favorable reputation preceded him. Ron's role was to identify growth opportunities for his company. He was a soloist, finding fertile sites where his company could set up shop profitably. Once he found them, he would work alone in those communities with neighbors, local governments, and businesses to cultivate grassroots support for his company's presence as a responsible corporate citizen and economic engine.

Ron and I had lunch. That's when I got an earful.

It turned out he was not at all happy with the way his company was treating him. He complained of getting little input on decisions he had to make, decisions that would have benefited from corporate guidance. His phone calls were not returned. His weekly activity reports were met with silence.

"Do they realize how many county and borough meetings I attend each month? How many miles I put on my car? How much indifference and undeserved antagonism I have to endure out here in the real world? How much blood, toil, tears, and sweat go into forging these community relationships?"

I could only tell him that I'd always heard his name mentioned with appreciation and respect. He wasn't hearing any of that.

"Yeah, well, that worked when I was younger and more impressionable, but this is getting to be a drag."

After another thirty minutes of accounts and remonstrations, Ron was unburdened.

"Please keep this to yourself." he said. "If I want this to go upstairs, I'll take it there myself."

As we parted company, I felt sure he was saying, "Nothing would make me happier than to tell those guys in corporate that I have another job, and it's all because of them! I'll go to them when I have that opportunity!"

A few weeks later, I was meeting with the senior executive to whom Ron reported. There were other issues that had brought us together that day, but during a break I mentioned that I'd met Ron, and I asked how the executive thought the lone ranger was doing.

"Ron's a treasure. We'd be lost without him."

"Really? In what way?"

The executive was animated. "He's closing in on a deal now that will pay off for years to come. He found it, nurtured it, is winning over the reluctant constituencies, and is now just months from bringing it all to fruition."

"Hmm, that's impressive! Does *he* know how much he's appreciated?"

"Well, he should! And if he doesn't he soon will, because when this project is sealed, I plan to give him a significant raise and bonus."

I strained to sound as casual as I could: "I wouldn't wait to give him some sign of your appreciation. This guy is working alone out there with a lot on his shoulders. Raises and bonuses are important, but I suspect he'd benefit from hearing your words of support and confidence."

I was prepared to leave it at that – Ron had specifically requested that I keep his confidence – but my advice was contrary to the executive's plans, and he wanted to continue discussing it.

"Really?" he asked with a vaguely dismissive tone. "I don't like to do that. I prefer to reward my people when they reach the zenith."

He'd opened the door, so I strolled in. I asked him to imagine that Ron was running a marathon. Marathoners don't need encouragement at the end of their 26.2 miles. Their sense of personal satisfaction (and maybe exhaustion) deafens them to recognition and congratulations from anyone else. Having achieved their goal, they are focused inward. But at mile fourteen, when their muscles are aching, their lungs burning, and their mind is playing tricks – that's when a marathoner's resolve can be replenished by a supporter along the route shouting words of encouragement and reminders that the quest is worth the enormous effort.

He listened carefully and said nothing (always a hopeful sign). As we returned to the meeting and were taking our seats, I caught his eye and whispered, "Ron is at mile fourteen."

This executive believed that results should be rewarded; efforts should be expected. Imagine him coaching his child's soccer team: he sits impassively, arms folded, cheering only when his team scores a goal. If the team wins, he buys them ice cream. If not, he drives them home. How'd you like your son or daughter playing for him? How'd you like to work for him? And while we're at it, how many runners do you have on your team at mile fourteen?

Like many things in life, your management relationship is strongest when it's balanced. Recognizing progress and effort doesn't ever diminish the impact of rewards for results.

PATIENCE: RECOGNIZING THE SMALL STEPS

When you're a graduate student in psychology, they have you work with rats, pigeons, and undergraduates. Somehow the powers that be figured out that if you can master those three species, all the others should be a piece of cake. It turns out I was really good with rats – put those little buggers in a maze and zap 'em with a low dose of electricity when they went the wrong way. Something about the concept made sense to me. So I moved on to pigeons with confidence and a bounce to my step. After all, I'd be that much closer to working with real people.

I remember the species transition vividly. It's all painfully easy to relive.

My professor congratulates me on my rat work and assigns me a laboratory pigeon. I name her Sylvia, after my grandmother. Sylvia is in a wire mesh cage about three feet wide by three feet tall by three feet deep. Less than luxurious accommodations. The cage has a round plastic disk on one wall, about pigeon-head high. My task is to train Sylvia to peck that disk. A food dispenser is right below the disk with an electric wire connected to it and to a handheld push button at the other end. If I press the button whenever Sylvia does what I want her to, a pellet of food drops into the dispenser where she can easily eat it.

For those of you who have not spent much time with pigeons, understand that they have a natural pecking instinct. They peck to eat, they peck to explore, they peck to fight, they even peck as they walk. So I don't have to teach Sylvia how to peck, just where and when. I remember thinking, "Sylvia pecks the disk, I reward her with a pellet, she gets the idea, and my professor releases me from the laboratory to work with undergraduates. Piece of cake."

It's a boiled-down metaphor for managing: I'm the boss who motivates Sylvia to perform a task. If she's successful, I'm successful. I even get a promotion.

The experiment begins. I stand over Sylvia with push button under my thumb, urging her to peck the disk. I speak softly and point at the disk with my finger. Sylvia has a different take on the matter. She's concerned only about this strange, hulking mass of humanity waving a finger and making noises above her...probably too nervous to think about food, never mind peck a disk.

Some time passes, and nothing good is happening. Despite my exhortations, Sylvia is not moving anywhere near that disk. In fact, Sylvia is not moving much at all. She's rigid and still. After forty five minutes, I'm no longer standing over her cage cheerleading like a helicopter parent at a Little League game. I'm sitting at my desk a few feet from the cage, working on a research paper for another class. I figure if Sylvia pecks the disk, I'll throw a pellet at her. Or maybe not. Frankly, I'm mad at Sylvia. I have places to go, a dissertation to write, professors to impress, and this bird is standing in my way.

After a few frustrating days of nonperformance despite my shouting, rattling, and imploring, I grab the cage with Sylvia inside and walk briskly up two flights of stairs from the laboratory to my professor's office. Barging in, I extend the cage to her and announce, "I need a new pigeon. This one doesn't work!" (Have you ever felt that way about an employee?)

My professor's response is calm, succinct, and thoroughly unsympathetic. "Let me remind you, sir, that the task here isn't to train the pigeon; it's to train you." (A memorable line if there ever was one.) "I'd urge you to reconsider which one of you isn't working. A little patient observation might do you some good. It might also help to remember what it took for you to learn how to walk and talk."

Back to the lab – to the dungeon – the cage in my arms, my tail between my legs. I position Sylvia on her shelf, reconnect the wire to the food dispenser, pull up a chair, and watch. A few things occur to me: First, Sylvia has to be hungry. She hasn't pecked the disk, and I haven't fed her. Second, she isn't as disturbed by my presence as she had been, no longer frozen in place. Third, as she moves more freely about her cage, she occasionally walks right by that disk.

I decide whenever she gets close, I'm going to give her a pellet. All I want is close – not looking for perfection anymore. Sure enough, when Sylvia's head nears the disk, I push my button. She hears the pellet drop and grabs it. In no time, she begins to hover near the disk. After just a few more pellets, she's actually hanging out right by the disk, probably thinking, "Good things happen when I'm over here."

I also notice that I have to feed her just when her head's within pecking range of the target. If I press my button after she's brushed by the disk and is headed toward a corner of the cage, she'll misinterpret the reinforcement and return to the corner. If I delay with the good stuff, I send the wrong message.

Eventually, more by accident than anything else, Sylvia's beak actually makes contact with the disk. She's pecked it! I hit that pushbutton as fast as my thumb can click. Sylvia gets a handful of pellets. I eat a couple myself!

Sylvia quickly becomes an enthusiastic pecker. In the process, she teaches me the concept of "successive approximations." I learn to catch her doing the task "approximately right," then "almost right," then "exactly right." A "C" performance is OK at the beginning. If I let Sylvia know that in a timely way, it leads to a "B" and eventually an "A". I'm not waiting for her to get to the zenith before recognizing her achievements.

We humans are not so different from pigeons. It's the rare employee who gets it right from the start. An administrative assistant who is tentative with a new technology won't master it overnight, even if the manual is perfectly clear. A staff member who has to make presentations to groups won't perfect eye contact, cadence, and voice control after watching a training DVD, studying an experienced speaker, or delivering one or two presentations herself. An unassertive engineer doesn't become assertive with customers in a single burst. An overbearing salesperson doesn't become charming after a heart to heart over lunch. Rome isn't built in a day. It's built by successive approximations...one peck at a time.

DIFFERENT SPECIES, DIFFERENT PELLETS

If the pigeon allegory is too simplistic for you, think about one of your kids. She gets a failing grade on a test. You're disappointed. Maybe you're furious. The two of you talk; or you yell, and she cries and yells back. Eventually you make it clear that more time has to be devoted to homework and conscientious studying. She agrees to give it her best shot. It helps that you've taken away everything she owns with a computer chip or battery in it.

You check in on her progress each night. You work with her. Rather than yell each time she claims she has to go to the bathroom or gazes vacantly out the window, you compliment her for at least being in the vicinity of her books (her disk). "You hung in there for forty-five minutes. That's a solid effort." A pellet.

Soon the next quiz looms, and you review the material together. For an hour. You can see she's struggling – she doesn't have it down – but at least she's aiming in the right direction.

"This isn't easy stuff, and I know you're trying, so do the best you can." Another pellet of recognition.

She takes the quiz, gets the grade, reports back to you. A "C." Do you rip into her for not getting an "A"? Do you yell at her for not studying hard enough? Criticize her for not taking her homework seriously? Rampage through her room in search of concealed electronics? Or do you smile, give her a hug and say, "You're making progress." (Remember, the last exam was an "F") "I'm proud of you. Let's keep up your study schedule, and you'll get even better grades. Here, sweetheart, have another pellet."

SETTING THE STAGE FOR INCREMENTAL SUCCESS

If school-age children seem more to you like undergraduates than real life employees, consider Art, a bright, eager manager in a manufacturing company. Art's superiors had directed him to do some research on U.S. firms that were producing state-of-the-art manufacturing technology. They wanted him to identify cutting edge equipment and software that could catapult the company to a leadership position in the industry. He was handed a significant budget to make the necessary purchases and then have his team lead the implementation.

A major corporate investment was on his shoulders, and it made him sweat. He would have to make the right purchase decisions, and his team would have to master the product suite to prove the money had been well spent. He was aware that the entire corporation – and the entire industry – would be watching.

Once Art and his key staff made the deal with their vendors, they planned their rollout to his technical team. To Art's credit, he was aware of his own anxiety. He knew it would undermine success if his employees suffered the brunt of it. He would have to find an alternative to nervously nagging for instantaneous perfection just to prove to the world that he'd made the right choices.

After carefully thinking through his strategy, Art made the team's challenge digestible for them in a kick-off presentation. "We're going to learn these new skills and begin applying them immediately. I'm looking forward to all of us being OK at this stuff in sixty days, good at it in 120 days and really excellent in 180 days so we can put it into full operation in all our plants."

His demeanor and his rallying cry set an achievable standard: OK to good to excellent within a manageable time frame. Next, he began to watch and learn from his staff which parts of the new technology came easily and which parts would require some trial and error, some software rewrites, and maybe some additional training resources from the vendors. Art was essentially managing everyone's expectations, including his own.

In the first two months, Art attributed employee errors and missteps to the learning curve rather than inadequacy. He was determined to recognize their progress rather than pounce on their failures. When a group of employees complained about how difficult the process was and pushed to extend the time required, Art was ready with reassurances: "Look, we're still in the early innings. We're still learning and finding the technical glitches. So we're meeting expectations. Yeah, it's challenging, but let's see it through."

The team did see it through. In successive approximations. It would have never gone down this way had Art let his anxiety get the best of him and his team.

SUCCESS IS NOT GUARANTEED

I had no such reasonable expectations for Sylvia. I began my experiment with a classic attitude: "You're a professional pecker, Sylvia! And I'm paying you for those pecks! Either perform, or I'll find someone who will!"

Of course this is not to say your patience with employees should – or can – be limitless. You're not a member of the clergy. You're not running a therapeutic community for employees. You're employer isn't paying you to be unconditionally nonjudgmental.

Realistically, there are pigeons, children, and employees that "don't work," that don't make it, even when you've set clear

expectations and provided constructive feedback and lots
of pellets. For a host of reasons – biochemical, emotional,
psychological, and intellectual – some people's skills, aptitudes,
and motivations simply aren't meant for the challenges of a
given job. Remember Brent's transfer to another department
because he lacked a technical and analytical bent?

But too frequently, managers are overcome by pressures, from
within or without, and they abandon the process of successive
approximation well before they've exhausted its potential.
They abandon it because they're diverted by their own failure
anxiety, or they've prejudged their employees. They get
frustrated with the pace of progress, or they cave under the
unrealistic expectations of their bosses. Many managers give up
because they simply don't believe that praising an employee's
progress has much effect. They don't believe that their signs
of approval can create influential moments in the management
relationship.

No words can adequately express my gratitude for the
teachings and guidance of my supervisor in graduate school.
His praise came so sparingly that one student described him as
"having been toilet trained with barbed wire." But when I did
something especially well, his tight-lipped smile and brief nod
made my heart soar. Whenever this brilliant but thoroughly
noneffusive mentor treated me to one of those "slips of
approval," I knew I had done well. And I knew it because I was
so keenly attuned to his passing expressions and gestures. It's
exactly the same with every one of your employees. There is
enormous power in moments of management approval. Even
the passing ones. They watch you like a hawk. They want to
make you smile.

CLARITY MAKES IT MORE INSTRUCTIVE

"Well done, Peggy." "Good work, Janice." "I'm really proud
of you, Herb." "Heck of a job, Brownie!" These are always

encouraging words, but they're not always as useful as they can be.

Words this general will make an employee feel good. But too often they don't communicate *what he or she should feel good about.* They're too broad to convey what the employee did to earn them.

Recognition can instill more than a positive feeling. It can be instructive. It can help an employee develop specific abilities and perspectives. To make it useful, you need to speak in words that your employee can "see." Being specific is powerful, whether you're catching an employee doing something right or wrong. You have to clear your head, formulate your thoughts, know exactly what you saw or heard or read that you want to recognize and encourage.

Obviously, there are exceptions, usually in nonwork settings. When your loved one puts an evening meal on the dinner table, imagine saying something like, "Oh, this looks beautiful! The juices pooling on the steak as the steam gently rises; the way you've arranged the green peas and orange carrots for an appetizing color scheme. I really love that rounded pat of yellow butter atop the carrots. Every detail makes this a wonderfully attractive and appealing presentation. *Bon appétit,* my dear!"

This is not how couples talk to each other. It's not how people communicate in 50/50 relationships. It's not affirming or instructive; it's verbose, overdone, and odd.

But when you speak with your employees, specifics are helpful. And motivating. Employees, new and seasoned, want to know what you value, and they discover it by what you recognize and praise. So you need to know what you value and how to articulate it.

Some managers have no expectations other than what their bosses prescribe: "This is what the boss wants." or "They say we have to do it this way." These managers are empty vessels with no internal values. Think for a moment what impact this approach would have on you as a subordinate. How much regard would you have for a managerially bankrupt boss?

Some managers project a strong, silent persona: "If you don't hear from me, assume you're doing fine. I'll let you know if you screw up." If you're like Ron, the business development guy at the top of this chapter, you're looking for another job.

And as I've said, some managers use only the broadest brush when they have something nice to say. "Nice job, Sam." More often than you may think, Sam is left with a question: "What exactly did I do that was a nice job?"

Most employees won't ask that question. Which means they're vulnerable to misinterpretations. So as time passes, they're repeating what they think you said they did well, and you're wondering why they aren't repeating what you said they did well! It's just like Sylvia heading for the corner instead of the disk because you fed her the pellet too late. The message wasn't precise enough. And whose fault do you suppose that is?

The manager who seizes the moment to describe what he *sees* is the manager who has the greatest positive impact on his management relationships. Imagine if the manager in the following situations just said, "Nice job." Would the moment be as instructive?

> "Paul, I realize it's not easy for you to pose those challenging questions about this project to your own colleagues, but I'm glad you did it in today's meeting. It makes us all sharper."

> "Diane, I know you would have liked more time to review the proposal, but I appreciate your decision to release it now so we have a shot at making our deadline."

> "Michael, thanks for dealing with that issue with Tim off line. It would have been distracting for the team if you'd taken time in the meeting."

> "Sam, today's presentation was a vast improvement. I liked the scenario you began with and how your summary wrapped your points up simply and clearly."

Sylvia pecked for pellets. Your children may be encouraged by a warm hug. Your employees will learn most from vivid words of recognition and encouragement.

As for taking the time to get good at this management skill, there's one more thing to consider:

Your employees will be able to digest more forthright criticisms if you've conveyed both a readiness and an ability to recognize what they do well. Praise is not just "nice." Nor is it just "motivating." It actually positions a manager to critique more candidly if and when a moment of instructive discomfort is called for.

An idea not coupled with action will never get any bigger than the brain cell it occupied.

~Arnold Glasow

CHAPTER SEVEN: CREDIBLE MOMENTS

Your management relationships are defined more by the disconnects your employees see than by the declarations they hear

Throughout this book I've emphasized that most managers underestimate how influential their fleeting moments of engagement with employees are. Too often, managers don't recognize that their relationships are forged in these moments.

But let me not leave you with the impression that everything of importance happens inside these moments. No matter how artfully you orchestrate a given interaction, it alone won't ensure the success of your management relationships. You're in the invisible spotlight between interactions, too. During these periods, your employees are looking for signs of your credibility. They're judging if you mean what you say. They're comparing word and deed. They're following your lead, not just your lips.

> "Did he mean it when he said he wanted my input on how to tackle this new research project?"
>
> "Is she really going to let me take the reins on this pricing policy revision?"
>
> "Will she have our backs during the corporate merger?"

"Will she stand up to the Budget Office on these program cuts like she said she would?"

"Could he really be willing to give me a second chance even though I let that relationship with one of our larger customers go south?"

A lot goes on in the passing moments. And a lot goes on between them, too, when employees get a glimpse of how closely what you say aligns with what you do. You can rest assured that your management relationships will be defined far more by the disconnects your employees see than by the declarations they hear.

THE CARING CULTURE

Frances worked hard, earned her promotion to director and, once in the position, continued her tireless pursuit of perfection. She was smart and driven and wanted very much to please her superiors.

Frances inherited control of a disorganized and ineffectual department. Over time, she gave that organization purpose, structure, and an enviable reputation throughout the company. She rightly believed her unyielding insistence on detailed procedures, thorough documentation, quantitative performance measures, and extensive administrative controls accounted for her department's success.

This company was growing rapidly, so my work involved consulting to its many new and newly promoted managers. The idea was to assure that each of them got off to a constructive and well-supported start. It was in this context that I met Frances and her staff.

To sustain her winning streak, Frances took it as her mission to eradicate departmental shortcomings of every kind. No plate was to hit the floor on Frances's watch. The fury and single-mindedness of her need for perfection were driving her staff and colleagues to sheer exhaustion.

Survival as an employee under Frances meant that every "i" had to be dotted, every "t" crossed. And everything – I mean everything – had to be approved by her. It was not uncommon for Frances's direct reports to endure hours in her office as she edited their written work, questioned their judgments and decisions, lectured them about her expectations, and subjected them to discussions about what they needed to do better or faster or more often or less often. It was punishing. And demeaning. And exhausting.

Appearances were important to Frances. She needed everyone in the company to believe her department was a high-functioning, well-oiled machine with productive and happy campers. She would wax eloquent in meetings with her boss and colleagues about the freedom to make independent decisions that she granted her subordinate managers. And Frances did indeed give her managers a wide berth…so long as they followed her every instruction. She would speak with pride about the open communication in her department. And it was indeed open…so long as people said exactly and only what Frances wanted to hear. She'd talk about how much pleasure her employees took in giving their all for the company. And they did…under threat of humiliating treatment for anything less.

Meanwhile, the parlor game among Frances's staff was figuring out how to avoid spending time with her, especially in closed-door meetings. In the best of times, a closed door signaled a prolonged deposition; in the worst of times, an interminable interrogation. These meetings would last for hours, sometimes well past the workday, until the prisoner confessed or lowered his head and surrendered to Frances's point of view. Her employees spent more time trying to figure out what Frances would accept than what would be best for the organization.

Consulting to Frances was a lot like reporting to her: withering. She was an ardent student of management theory, devouring all the latest and greatest management books. She came to our early conversations armed with compelling (if not somewhat twisted) justifications for her methods: "Aren't we supposed to stretch ourselves and our employees?" "Aren't I supposed to communicate clearly and directly when a subordinate falls short of expectations?" "Isn't it my obligation as a manager to coach and mentor my staff?" "Wasn't it *you* in our managers' meeting a few weeks ago who, as our consultant, advised us that setting standards and following up is critical to success?"

Frances couldn't grasp the idea that too much of a good thing can be destructive. She was like an intelligent thinker who uses too many twenty-five-cent words or a gifted musician who drowns out the rest of the orchestra. Frances used the tactics of productive management to counterproductive extremes.

Nonetheless, as a result of some of our discussions and the comments of a few of her colleagues in the Human Resources Department, Frances began to acknowledge signs – slowly and defensively – that all was not well in her department. The morale was not exactly soaring, and there were grumblings from within about how oppressive the environment was. As is sometimes the case, just as Frances began to see the chinks in her armor, she became less inclined to speak about them with others, including me. She prided herself on self-sufficiency and so was determined to tackle the issue alone. I saw no value in imposing myself; I directed my attention to other corporate issues, knowing that sooner or later Frances and I would be back in touch.

After combing through the management literature for the secrets of employee happiness, Frances called a meeting of her department's managers and supervisors. She asked them for suggestions on how morale could be improved. As you might expect, the discussion was awkward, halting, and drowning in polite obfuscation. No one said, "Frances, if you would just lighten up, things would be a lot better around here." Instead, the air was heavy with well-worn, safe, and hopelessly saccharine ideas about "team building," "taking ownership," and "trust."

Eventually, someone stumbled on the idea that "we should just care more."

Frances jumped on it. "We should care more...yes, we should create a 'Caring Culture'! That would be excellent." Everyone agreed quickly and enthusiastically. After all, it was getting near dinnertime.

Frances's mind was now locked on her target. She immediately began assigning people in the room to one of three task groups. The first would work on a definition of a Caring Culture. The second group would flesh out the measurement criteria for a Caring Culture. And the third would brainstorm ways for the department to "celebrate" a Caring Culture once one was achieved. Employees began averting their gaze and slumping in their chairs in desperate attempts to avoid being chosen. To no avail, of course.

In the days that followed, Frances was delighted that she'd hit the Management Trifecta. She had combined three ideas *du jour* into her program: Teamwork, Participative Management, and her very own Caring Culture. She couldn't wait to bring this brave new initiative to the attention of her boss and colleagues.

The Culture groups met once each week for several weeks to slog through their assignments. Frances attended every meeting so she could tell everyone what to say. By the end, the hallmarks of a Caring Culture had been codified. The Values and Guidelines were edited *ad nauseam* and finally printed in elaborate lettering on an enormous poster that hung prominently in the department's center aisle. The poster was titled "The Caring Culture Declaration." Frances organized a

Caring Ceremony in which all employees signed the poster as a token of their allegiance. And it was done.

THE COLLAPSE OF THE CARING CULTURE

Some weeks after the entire process had run its course, I went to visit Frances. I'd followed the progress of the Caring Culture from a distance, worried that it was exactly what Frances should not be doing. I wanted to see if my hunch was wrong, if the effort was indeed proving worthwhile. Stranger things have happened.

Frances was brimming with pride. No sooner had I taken a seat beside her desk than she asked me what I thought of the Caring Culture. This was difficult. How do you tell someone like Frances you think she's doused a skunk with perfume?

I paused for a moment and then asked, "Frances, if you wanted to create a Cursing Culture, how would you go about doing it?"

She laughed nervously. "I don't know what you mean." I asked the same question again, but she demurred once more, so I plunged ahead without her encouragement.

"If you wanted to create a Cursing Culture, you know what you'd do? You'd curse! You'd go to a meeting, and in the midst of answering a question or making a point you'd throw in an F-bomb. You'd follow up with a raunchy SOB and then a harsh G-D. In the days after, while tongues were still wagging about your colorful language, you'd put on a similar show in some other public setting. Curse often and publicly enough, and before you know it, you have yourself a lively Cursing Culture. Within no time your folks would be cursing like sailors on leave."

Frances was not pleased. But she was far too smart not to understand the moral of my story. Suggesting that her machinations were wasteful wasn't the worst of it. The worst of it was that I was holding up the consultant's mirror. And the mirror was reflecting a fatal disconnect between her proclamations about the Caring Culture and the demoralizing impact of her day-to-day management moments.

"Frances, the culture of your organization grows out of what you do as much as what you say. If you treat people as if they have minds of their own, as if they're adults, as if they're capable of making sound judgments and of learning from their mistakes, they'll appreciate that you care about their welfare and professional success, and they'll begin to 'care' themselves. They'll care about doing competent work; they'll care about contributing to their organization; they'll care as much as you do about the plates not dropping. They want to please you, Frances. You just don't give them the breathing room to try."

I wish I could report that Frances's eyes brightened as insight flooded her consciousness, but that was not to be. Soon after her grand scheme for a cultural revolution was in place, it became apparent that reality was grossly out of step with the promise. In fact, the charade did little more than calcify her employees' hard feelings toward her. This is the common outcome of hypocrisy.

Within a few months, Frances left her company for a job with another organization. It's doubtful she could have recovered from her bruised relationships even had she seen the light. Too much water under the bridge. But there's a lot the rest of us can learn from her experience.

Managers who jump on the latest and greatest organizational gimmick to camouflage their own inadequacies or to make favorable impressions on their bosses do so at their own risk. It's the credibility thing. It's like staging your house for sale by painting over the water-stained dry wall instead of repairing the leak.

Your employees watch you like a hawk, keenly observing what you say, how you say it, what you do, and how you do it. You cannot escape the invisible spotlight. And as childlike as you might think it is, they will imitate you, too. That's right: full-grown, levelheaded, self-respecting adults will imitate you. It's not childlike really. It's human. Keep your jacket on during meetings and others will follow your lead. Take that jacket off and observe how your employees interpret your action as permission to remove their own jackets. Wear a tie or a scarf to work each day and watch them begin to appear on others.

In a more substantive and important way, your employees adopt your point of view; they mimic your approach to people and to problems. If you're open to ideas and give the benefit of the doubt to others, your employees will do likewise. By the same token, if you're intolerant, accept nothing short of perfection, question the trustworthiness or speak ill of your colleagues, you'll hear echoes of these same attitudes in your employees' words and actions. Like the song says, "Teach your children well."

Employees act on the unspoken and near universal assumption that to be like you is to be liked by you. The enlightened manager with honorable intentions understands this dynamic and uses it to encourage the highest levels of pride and commitment.

CARING IN DEED

It should be noted that the idea Frances was trying to promote – the idea of an organization that's invested in its own excellence and the professional well-being of its members – is sound and worthy. There are simply far better ways for a leader to bring the idea to life.

I was listening to a sports channel on the car radio late one afternoon. The program was covering the retirement of the city's NFL coach. During his tenure, he had produced a fiercely competitive powerhouse, winning several divisional titles and earning its share of Super Bowl glory.

In one segment of the station's retrospective, a reporter interviewed current and retired players about their memories and reflections. A lineman who had played for the coach since college poignantly recounted a defining moment from his rookie year.

He began by divulging his early, private struggles adjusting to the league and to the team's defensive system. For him, the college football universe was nothing like the NFL, and the team's defensive strategies were forcing him to relearn everything he thought he knew about his position. His self-doubts were persistent enough that he asked for some time with the coach. As luck would have it, their first opportunity to talk was at the end of a long day's practice. They met in the parking lot on route to their respective cars.

The lineman confessed to the sports reporter that, without intending to, he unloaded every one of his pent-up concerns and doubts on the coach. He told the reporter he had been deeply grateful ever since for the coach's willingness to hear him out. But what touched him most, he said, was this:

> As we spoke, standing between parked cars in the lot by the practice field, it grew dark and started to rain. A light drizzle became a steady rain in a matter of minutes. And through it all, that man never budged, never flinched. Nothing seemed more important to him at that moment than understanding me and my woes. The coach stood by me during that difficult time in my career, and I have been proud to stand by him ever since.

A caring culture, or any kind of culture you try to foster in your organization, grows out of credible moments – moments in which your deeds say the same thing as your words. A "culture of excellence," an "entrepreneurial culture," a "data-driven culture," a "merit-based culture," a "customer-centric culture" – every single one of them depends on your consistency. When what you say and what you do convey the same message, your motives are believable and your management relationships strong.

It was when I found out I could make mistakes
that I knew I was on to something.

~Ornette Coleman

CHAPTER EIGHT:
MOMENTS OF RECOVERY

*Managing is a sloppy game with too many
unknowns to calculate the right moves every
time; recovering from a mistake is one of the
hardest challenges to address with grace*

Y ou can dedicate yourself to honoring every principle
and prescription in this book, and still you will stumble.
More than once in your career, you'll look dumb, give the
wrong impression, bruise someone's feelings, have a meltdown.
Everyone takes his or her eye off the ball once in a while.
Everyone is blind to some persistent idiosyncrasy or other that
spells management trouble.

If these eventualities are not what you bargained for as a
manager, go to your room and hide under your bed. You'll
make fewer blunders there.

While I'm at it, let me make the cruel truth even more so. If
you've been paying attention over the last seven chapters, you
know *they're* all paying attention to *you.* You're in that invisible
spotlight. Your employees are talking about you at the dinner
table, listening to what you say, measuring how closely your
words square with your deeds. So a management mistake is
always *under a more high-powered microscope* than a private or
personal one.

Skillful managers have learned that ignoring a misstep or
denying a destructive behavior pattern is itself destructive.
They've come to appreciate that a blown opportunity or

brainless act creates one more opportunity to strengthen the management relationship. Clearly, recovering from a mistake is one of the hardest challenges to address with grace. It takes more soul searching and intestinal fortitude than carrying out a routine management duty. But therein lies the chance to excel.

PICK YOURSELF UP, DUST YOURSELF OFF

Kathy was a newly made partner in a prestigious law firm. She was making the transition – the passage – from an associate who did everything for herself and for the firm's partners to a manager who dispatched associates and paralegals to do exploratory background work on her behalf. We met soon after she became a partner.

Mark was one of the firm's most impressive paralegals – assertive, eager to learn and to prove himself. Kathy decided that he was ready to interview witnesses for one of her cases. These interviews are a crucial step in building any sound legal case and a choice assignment for a paralegal. Mark was thrilled. She instructed him on the general approach to conducting this kind of interview and taking a written statement, a process she knew he'd observed in prior cases.

The paralegal impressed Kathy during their preparations. Believing that he had demonstrated sufficient legal sense and savvy, she mentioned a subtle maneuver for "locking in" witnesses to their statements. The interviewer would purposely record an insignificant detail incorrectly in the written statement. Then, during a review of the statement for accuracy, the witness would catch the error, correct it, and initial the correction. If the witness later changed any part of his statement on the stand, the attorney could refer to his initials as proof he had attested to the statement's accuracy and corrected any errors, implying that his testimony on the stand was suspect.

Mark appeared to understand the maneuver and its purpose, so Kathy didn't dwell on it.

After he conducted his first interview, Mark checked in with Kathy. He reported that things had gone well and gave her the signed statement with witness initials. He was beaming with pride, and she could see that. She read through the document while he sat across from her. As she turned the pages, her expression of interest turned to a frown and then to horror. She was discovering that Mark had not chosen a minor detail requiring the witness's correction, but a major one. The document made it appear that Mark had gotten the witness to change his story on a fact that was central to the entire case. It made the statement beyond worthless; it was now actually detrimental.

Kathy was visibly shaken. Angry and disappointed. At an octave or two higher than normal, she made clear how disastrous the situation was, and Mark was crushed by a sense of failure. He retreated from her office, and in the days that followed he went into hiding, skulking off to work with other partners whom he hoped had not heard about his blunder and Kathy's outburst.

Only when it became obvious that Mark was giving her a wide berth did Kathy realize she'd damaged him and their working relationship. She was deeply regretful. I wasn't surprised. I knew Kathy to be a decent human being who strove to do every part of her job honorably, including the management part. Puncturing the spirits of a colleague was not in her makeup.

Now she was concerned, not just about the fate of the case, but that Mark would caution the firm's other paralegals and associates about working with her. And he probably did. She worried that her ability to direct others would be questioned by her colleagues and senior partners. She knew that office grapevines are well watered.

The fact was, Kathy's exasperation in front of Mark had little to do with Mark and everything to do with herself. His error was the result of her incomplete guidance. She had discussed the technique with him as if he were a knowledgeable colleague, not a newbie. She had glossed over the importance of choosing a minor fact to transcribe incorrectly. She saw in hindsight that it would have been wiser to save this legal maneuver for when he had had more interview experience.

But in that moment of agitation, when it became apparent that the statement would undermine her case, she simply couldn't articulate any of this. She didn't mean to punish Mark. But that didn't matter. Her impact mattered. The blunder was hers. The recovery would need to be hers as well.

She thought carefully about what she wanted to say and do. Then she asked Mark to stop by her office. He came in sheepishly and stood by her desk. She stood as well. She told him she was sorry for having lit into him. "My behavior was uncalled for and personally embarrassing." She went on to say that her anger was really directed more at herself than Mark. She said there were two things she regretted. First, that she had not provided more precise directions; in retrospect, he could not possibly have known to handle the interview differently. And second, that her fury conveyed to Mark a loss of confidence in him. In fact, she thought he was one of the most talented paralegals in the firm, and her opinion hadn't changed. She concluded the conversation by telling him she hoped they could work together again in the future.

Kathy spoke the words that needed to be spoken. She began her recovery. If you've never been in her shoes, it's hard to appreciate the courage she mustered. Think about how easy it would have been for her to step past the casualty. All she'd need are a few standard managerial excuses, justifications, and self-delusions:

If he wasn't sure, he should have asked questions.

Somebody with his experience should have known better.

I'm a partner; I'm allowed to blow off steam once in a while.

If he can't take a little rough handling, he'll never make it in this firm.

But these would have been small-minded for Kathy. Not the style of any self-respecting manager committed to preserving work relationships. Her simple, unvarnished admission of responsibility was a far harder choice, but a far wiser one. You can be certain Mark heard every last word she spoke. Even as he struggled to believe she was put out only with herself and not with him, he respected and appreciated the unusual gesture of a partner apologizing to a paralegal.

Now only time and a clean record, free of blowups, would heal the wound. In the following weeks, Kathy intentionally engaged Mark. She assigned him important work, went over instructions and legal tactics with more care, critiqued his assignments evenhandedly, and assured him of his value and promise. As you might predict, over time her efforts paid off handsomely. Mark became the reliable, industrious, and insightful colleague she had sought to develop.

YOUR INTENTION IS NOT YOUR IMPACT

Now here's the truth: few employees believe gaffes like Kathy's are truly unintentional. They don't really buy the "just a bad day" thing. They believe at some level you mean those slips of the tongue or personal slights, no matter how well you quickstep after the fact.

Sometimes your employees are right about this. Sometimes they're wrong. But the thing is, your intentions don't matter. Your impact matters. All Mark knew was that Kathy had blown a gasket, and it made him believe he'd failed. Her intentions never entered his mind. That's why the burden fell to her to recover. She was responsible for this relationship and she was losing it. For Kathy, it was a priceless lesson about the management relationship.

BREAKING THE CHAINS OF HABIT

Kathy had to recover from a single, isolated incident. But what about the manager who inflicts repeated harm? What if the management relationship is damaged by chronic oversights or flaws? Is there a similar path to recovery?

Some years ago, I was asked by the CEO of an international solar energy company to consult with his vice president of European market development. Lou was a talented guy with a knack for turning up particularly promising acquisition opportunities. The CEO thought Lou's business development skills were exceptional. He was concerned, however, that Lou gave his management responsibilities short shrift, ignoring his obligation to develop his senior staff. This was a priority for the president. He believed there were capable deputies under Lou, but they weren't being challenged with responsibility. He expected Lou to fix that. I was dispatched to help him become as skillful a manager as he was a market developer.

I wanted to watch him in action, so Lou invited me on a one-week, whirlwind tour through Europe with his four deputies. The pace was frenetic and disorienting. We started with back-to-back prospect meetings in Holland, continued without a break through Italy and Spain, and finally landed in Frankfurt, Germany for morning-to-night negotiations.

Lou and I rented a private office in the Frankfurt airport to debrief in the hours before our separate flights – his back to Holland, mine home to the States. We took our seats in that stark gray office overlooking the tarmac and dispensed with small talk. Time was limited.

I'd watched him for an intense week, and I knew what my mirror had to show him. "Well, Lou, you certainly are a maestro. Across different languages, national customs, and a cobweb of organizational cultures, you were charming, curious, definitive, and always professional. You represented your company well; you're an exceptional ambassador. Frankly, I was captivated by your interactions and negotiations, especially because you handled them as if you had had far more sleep and preparation than I knew you'd had."

Lou was obviously pleased by the mirror's reflection. But I had more.

"On the other hand, you treated your deputies like a silent entourage, not like professionals with something of substance to contribute. You were pleasant and playful about it, but the message was unmistakable: your guys are window dressing; you like how they look, but you don't treat them as if they have much to contribute beyond enlarging your own presence. It surprised me. You yourself told me how much you thought each had to offer. My own conversations with them over the week seemed to confirm your assessment. Yet there was never much room for them in the action. You never consulted them, solicited their counsel, gave them an opportunity to demonstrate their worth. Because of that, they're tentative and subdued, convinced that expressing their ideas and opinions would be like trying to charge solar panels with a flashlight. You're getting far less from your staff than you could, far less than they want to offer."

Lou sat quietly for a moment and then argued with the skill and contained ferocity of a trained fencer. For the next forty minutes we lunged and feinted and parried. I explained what I saw and heard, offering example after example. He deflected every one, protesting that I simply hadn't seen enough to understand his management relationships. We argued back and forth until we were exhausted, staring out at the tarmac, wishing our flights were earlier so we could excuse ourselves from the awkward silence.

After we'd been in our corners for a few minutes without a word, Lou turned back to me. His sword was down, his tone more conciliatory. "I guess you're telling me my socks smell."

All I could do was sigh deeply. "You're going to have to explain that one to me."

"When I go home to my family after a busy week like this, we all sit around the living room talking or watching TV together. My wife and I sit in our big double chair, my four kids huddle around us. I take my shoes off and put my feet up on our ottoman. And like clockwork, the kids start moaning that my socks smell. I tell them, 'Listen, I'm the dad, the head of this household. You'll just have to deal.'

"That's what you're telling me. My employees think my socks smell, and I know they do, and I don't care."

I agreed and asked him what I often ask managers with smelly socks: "What do you want those four guys thinking? What would you want them saying it's like to work for Lou?"

He thought about it before answering. "I'd want them to think of me the way you said my prospects and clients think of me: charming, attentive, curious, and all the rest. And I'd certainly like my boss hearing that's what my guys think."

"You already have the skills you need, Lou. It's a matter of seeing the payoff in managing your employees as attentively as you do your prospects. If you can get your head around that, you'll be in business."

With that, my work was done for the moment. We headed for our separate gates.

Lou shared the gist of our conversation with only two people: his wife and his CEO. No doubt he told his wife expecting that she'd confirm the need for him to make some changes. He told his boss to assure him that he was now aware of the problem and intent on solving it.

Exactly two weeks after our airport conversation, Lou's senior-most deputy tendered his resignation. He said he had been offered a position elsewhere in which his "knowledge and skills would be more fully put to use." It confirmed the CEO's worst fears about Lou. When they spoke about it – and the CEO issued an ultimatum – Lou's awareness of the problem became a crusade to recover from the damage he'd done. He could no longer take his work relationships for granted as if he were the "head of the household." It was now Lou who would have to deal.

His gradual recovery was an exercise in humility and discipline. Everything he had to do defied the very instincts that brought him to this point in his career. He was learning to keep his shoes on and more conscientiously manage his deputies. He practiced soliciting their ideas, sharing the stage with them, offering counsel and support. His deputies took notice, but they were hesitant to put any stock in it.

Part of what makes recovering so difficult for managers – aside from pride and inflexibility – is the suspicion of those who have been injured or slighted. The truth is, most employees just don't believe you can change. If your "nature" is tyrannical, neglectful, slick, duplicitous or whatever – and you're lucky enough to be made aware of it – your recovery is up against a deep skepticism in your employees.

You must expect this, not bemoan it or be defeated by it: your reputation will change more slowly than your behavior, no matter how earnest your intentions. The people around you need to see credible evidence of a change. That takes time.

Several months later, Lou lost a second deputy, but this time to a transfer that had nothing to do with his management approach. The result actually accelerated his improvements. It gave him an opportunity to hire a second new employee. His two new staff members had no history with him, so they had no reason to second-guess the impressions he made. Lou was eager to engage them, he gave them responsibility for critical projects, and he made sure they were paid well and well-respected. They had no reason to question his authenticity.

That's how recovering your work relationships goes when bad habits have to be reengineered. Sometimes the wind is behind your sails and propels you forward. Lou had the advantage of an insistent boss, our fencing match in the airport, the wake-up call of a resignation, and the opportunity for a fresh start with new deputies. Frankly, this is rare. Many managers don't recover like Lou did. When it comes to chronic blind spots and harmful idiosyncrasies, recovery is a much harder challenge. Sometimes it's insurmountable. When the patience and trust of your employees are tested beyond their limits, the mountain can become too steep and slippery. If it does, the only answer is to step aside and start anew.

To his credit, Lou took advantage of his good fortune. He worked hard to become a better manager; far from perfect, but more adept. He had good days and bad. Some years later, he and I passed in the Chicago airport. We quickly caught each other up since our time together years earlier in another busy terminal. As we said our farewells and turned to get to our respective flights, Lou shouted after me, "You know, I still think about my socks." Earlier that month, Lou had assumed the CEO position with a large company.

THERE IS NO UNDO COMMAND

You can't take back a management *faux pas*. And there's no Delete key for the even greater harm of a chronic bad habit. In the same way you can't undo a physical injury, you can't rewrite your management history.

So what do you do once you've fallen off the ladder, injuring yourself and maybe someone below? If you're smart, you step up to your obligation to apologize and make reparations to your victims. You resolve to climb ladders in the future with more care. And if the injury leaves your body permanently compromised, you stay off ladders.

It's exactly the same when you try to recover from management injuries – those you inflict and those you sustain. You apologize and begin rebuilding the foundation of your relationship with care. The way to do this is by *compensating for the damage you've done in a compelling way*. Though you can't take back a slap in the face, you can stop slapping – and offer enough evidence of regret, respect, and reform to dilute the impact.

The best you can do is offset the offense. Balance the ledger. Recovery is a matter of creating enough positive moments in the management relationship to restore your credibility and the goodwill of your employees.

PART III:
MANAGEMENT PASSAGES

You seldom sit at a crossroads
and know it's a crossroads.

~Alex Raffe

CHAPTER NINE: THE CROSSROADS

Learning that your staff's achievements reflect on you, rather than displace you, can be one of your toughest and most enduring management lessons

Progressing through your management career is all about adapting to changing situations. You have to master new tasks, develop new relationships, and assume new responsibilities. It's not just a matter of acquiring skills the way you acquire a new car. It's more complicated than that. It's a matter of *overlaying new skills on your old habits*. And as we all know, old habits die hard. Especially those habits that have brought you rewards and gratifications.

Those of you who have been exceptional employees are acutely aware of this struggle. Your successes were achieved by *doing* things. By *executing*. When you became a manager, you were expected to *do* less and *direct* more. You were expected to delegate, to teach, to support. These aren't just new ways of behaving; they are in direct conflict with the *impulse to perform*.

Every competent manager learns how to make this transition eventually, but it's not without an internal struggle. As you would expect, the struggle is most acute in times of crisis. Dan, a favorite client, is a case in point. He's yet another example of how sustained, conscious effort is indispensable to mastering the management role.

THE SUPERSTAR SYNDROME

When I first met Dan, he was a rookie manager in the fast lane: bright, driven, articulate, appealing, and effective. Dan had executive potential written all over him. He was an impact player in his organization whose gifts would no doubt land him in a position of significant influence one day. He carried himself with intensity and a natural urgency that encouraged those around him to move things forward and bring issues to resolution.

Like many fast-track managers, Dan's greatest assets in some situations played out as liabilities in others. He fought his natural tendency to run over people in meetings, to grab control from those he thought were dawdling or just idling. He had the answers well before others knew what the questions were, a source of unending frustration for him. In his youth, Dan had been a formidable gymnast. These days he was a disciplined long-distance runner. He had competitive fire in his eyes and a desire to surpass whatever goals were set, no matter how demanding.

I enjoyed my consulting conversations with Dan. He was open to suggestions and eager to think in new ways about the role and responsibilities of management. Most impressive, he had an observing ego, a capacity to assess his impact from the viewpoint of others. He had an intuitive awareness of the invisible spotlight. He understood how his strengths helped him and how they could trip him up. He never gave our discussions short shrift and strove to put into action the management strategies we would flesh out together.

Our earliest consultations were about the basic challenge of managing versus doing – accomplishing things through his management relationships instead of doing it all himself.

BABY STEPS

For superstars, giving up center stage doesn't come naturally. For Dan, the challenge of this shift in attitude and behavior can't be overstated. He often felt like an alcoholic in recovery – purposely taking detours to avoid the neighborhood bar. But he practiced holding back his points of view until his employees had expressed theirs first. He practiced asking questions that would encourage employees to think more clearly and more imaginatively. He forced himself to select the best of his employees' ideas – even if they had less sparkle than his own – so his staff would know their contributions were worthy and valued. He was gradually becoming a purposeful manager. He discovered that cultivating an environment in which his group could succeed brought its own rewards.

As was typical of the way we worked, I stopped in on Dan unannounced one morning.

"You're going to be mad a me." he said.

Our relationship had evolved to the point where discussions had no formal beginning, middle, or end. Whenever we met, we'd simply pick up midstream, wherever there were rocks or currents that Dan needed to navigate. Pleasantries and context were unnecessary.

"Why will I be mad at you?"

"Because next week, I'm going on vacation with my wife. We're going to Europe."

"Nothing to be mad at so far."

"And I plan to call in every morning at 7:30 local time to run a staff meeting."

Alarm bell. This would be a setback…a vestige of Dan's need to be in the fray.

Or maybe not. There was the fact that Dan chose to share his plans with me. This suggested that he knew he was about to act unwisely. He surely knew I would think there were better alternatives. I suspected he was looking for one as we sat across from one another in his office.

I suggested to him that a boss's vacation provides invaluable opportunities for employees, not the least of which is that they get a vacation from the boss! "When you return, Dan, your employees get to impress you with how well they've handled things while you were gone. Calling in every morning to control the show will rob them of these opportunities and belittle their capabilities at the same time. Your long-distance staff meetings will sabotage the progress you've made the last few months. Those conference calls will be saying to your staff, 'If the place goes up in flames, I'm the only competent firefighter around here. When push comes to shove, my management development – and your growth as employees – is a fair weather game.' "

Dan listened. He always did. He tried to reconcile his conflicting intentions. But he must have devoted a few sleepless nights to preparing a rationale for his daily transatlantic telecommutes because he then delivered a round of well-constructed arguments. Like a defense attorney stalking the jury box, he rose from his chair, paced his office, orating more than conversing.

He explained that there were critical issues swirling through the company; had he known they were coming to a head during his vacation week, he never would have scheduled Europe in the first place. He was certain that without his guidance and oversight, his unseasoned supervisory staff simply was not ready to make the key judgments and decisions that would come up during his week away. Through no fault of their own, he feared they would be lost in his absence. The organization would suffer. This would represent an intolerable situation as far as he was concerned.

It was a powerful performance. His reasoning was sound. His willingness to sacrifice his vacation out of devotion to the business, even at the expense of his wife's enjoyment, was simultaneously impressive and unsettling.

Only one thing overshadowed the irresistible force of Dan's eloquent case: I had heard it all before. He'd tried to foist the same logic on me on other occasions, when no vacations loomed and no critical corporate issues hung in the balance.

The truth of it was, Dan just didn't want to be left out of the action. Were he on hand in a crisis, he knew he'd be able to dive into a telephone booth at a moment's notice and change into his Superstar costume. But a distance of six thousand miles would make heroic acts impossible.

I told him it was unlikely that his company would forget him or penalize him for taking a vacation. And I made clear that he had within his repertoire both the professional discipline and the management smarts to resist his craving for daily, hands-on involvement.

THE CROSSROADS

Dan was at a crossroads. He knew time was limited, and the challenge would be substantial. He thoroughly dreaded the consequences should his staff misstep while he was vacationing. I assured him that the supervisors who report to him were as prone to errors as he dreaded. And I reminded him that he had for some time been resolved to confront the challenges of his transition from doing to leading. This would be a pivotal one.

Dan was beginning to see the vacation not as a missed opportunity to prove his individual worthiness, but as a chance to demonstrate his *management* worthiness. The trip would allow him to test – and showcase – the leadership talents he had been working so hard to nurture in his staff. He also knew that engineering this moment capably would impress those whose opinions he cared about and respected.

ABSENCE MAKES THE EMPLOYEE GROW FASTER

Now the focus of our conversation shifted from, "How can I stay in contact during my vacation without undermining my staff?" to "How do I prepare my team in this very short time to be smart and responsive while I'm enjoying the delights of Paris?"

In the week that followed, Dan met with his employees individually and in small groups to outline the possible scenarios and to designate who among them would take the lead. He briefed them on the guidance and assistance they could depend on from other managers if things got confusing or out of hand. He met with his counterparts to lay out how he had deployed his staff and to whom he'd assigned responsibilities. He ran a joint meeting of employees and his colleagues to cement these connections. Finally, he chatted with his boss.

Dan's manager assured him that he should take and enjoy his vacation. He let her know that he was heartbroken to hear he was expendable. She told him it was all his fault; after all, he was the one doing what needed to be done to assure his dispensability for a week. She also wanted him to know that the thinking he was doing and the steps he was taking to prepare his staff were the subject of discussion among her colleagues. She confided that it had caused her to rethink some of her own practices.

If Dan harbored any lingering doubts about giving his supervisory staff the elbow room to manage the week without his close supervision, they were vaporized by his boss's words of genuine support and admiration.

THE REWARDS OF SELF-RESTRAINT

I caught up with Dan a few weeks later. His vacation was a success in a variety of ways. He and his wife had a wonderful time, there were no calamities or casualties at work, and no one begrudged his absence or forgot his name. None of the things he most feared came to fruition.

He was quick to confess that he'd called in that week, but only once. "You couldn't expect me to go cold turkey!" But he'd used that call to check in, not to take over. He had confined himself to listening, praising, and encouraging his staff, not flooding them with directions.

When he returned, he found that his employees had performed admirably in his absence, some more adroitly than others. Several had war stories to tell, and some bragged about their successes and the compliments they'd received.

In the days after he got back, he sensed an increased level of enthusiasm and commitment within the team as they handled day-to-day details that he had previously kept for himself. He also noted that a number of the issues being brought to his attention by his supervisors were more sophisticated because the staff was beginning to dispose of the more routine matters themselves. He was responding by delegating broader responsibilities to those on the team who had demonstrated a capacity to take them on and who had earned the trust of his fellow managers.

MANAGEMENT IS WORK

Does Dan's story sound too good to be true? Too easy? Too perfect? Well, while it's a gratifying and instructive success story, it was far from easy and by no means perfect. I can say this with confidence because almost ten years later, Dan and I still stay in touch with one another. Today, he's a vice president. A good one at that. But he'd be the first to say he's had setbacks, self-doubts, and sometimes an impossible time containing his appetite for center stage. *Overlaying new skills on insistent old habits isn't as simple as buying a new car.*

Becoming a manager is a far more dramatic transition than most people realize. It goes well beyond the raise, the new office, and the hearty congratulations from co-workers, friends, and family. Becoming a manager profoundly alters your outlook on work, your image of yourself, your impact on others, and the ways you seek professional satisfaction.

In truth, the crossroads that most managers face isn't nearly as stark and dramatic as Dan's. His came at a time when his management education was already well under way. He was already actively exploring the role and was committed to mastering it. The vacation was just a more vivid fork in the road than most: one path leading to the tried and true glories of frontline heroism, the other to the less familiar glories of training heroes.

You'll confront your crossroads in less exaggerated circumstances. Your fork won't be as clearly marked, the paths not as sharp edged, your decisions less conscious and considered. But in countless passing moments, you'll make your choice. The question is, will your choice be dictated by what's comfortable for you, or by what's best for your management relationships and your own professional growth?

Dan had to make a concerted effort to forego center stage. As he set out for his vacation, he was satisfied that he'd done all he could to prepare his employees for the week. He also had to make a leap of faith that his staff could succeed and that their success would reflect on him rather than displace him. It's the same kind of discipline that all of us have to put into subduing our old habits to make room for new skills.

For every complex problem there is an
answer that is clear, simple, and wrong.

~H. L. Mencken

CHAPTER TEN:
WHEN THE MAGIC DOESN'T SEEM TO WORK

Sometimes your plate gets full with unwanted developments, imperfect choices, and unexpected outcomes.

There are times when your employees drive you crazy. There are times you'll do everything "right" and still the outcome won't be what you want or expect. It's just the way it is.

Management relationships do not lend themselves to scientific precision. I've underscored your responsibility to create the *conditions for employee success.* That's what a healthy, productive management relationship does. *But you're not responsible for the success of every employee.*

It's a crucial distinction. Not every employee is suited to every job. As I mentioned in chapter 6, there are pigeons, children, and employees who won't make the grade, even when you've set clear and reasonable expectations, provided training and constructive feedback, and dispensed lots of pellets. Some people's temperament, aptitudes, and motivations just aren't meant for the challenges of a given job, even when you create an environment designed to help them succeed.

Put another way, there are many factors beyond the management relationship itself that determine an employee's success. Your objective is to preserve a basic level of respect, confidence, and goodwill in that relationship – *whether the employee's performance is good or bad; whether you're welcoming him on his first day of work, or escorting him out the door on his last.*

HOW DO YOU SPELL MANAGEMENT RESPONSIBILITY?

Jen was a capable manager at a university-affiliated hospital. Her staff was proud to work for her, her boss knew she would always deliver, and her colleagues respected her contributions and commitment to the hospital's mission.

Josh was one of Jen's employees. His job in records management required organization and prompt responsiveness to the hospital's professional staff. Josh was a young man at the dawn of his career, a recent college graduate with soaring self-esteem and boundless expectations for rapid advancement. Unfortunately his discipline and sense of urgency weren't equal to his self-assurance. Jen liked his drive and energy, but the accuracy and timeliness of his work left much to be desired. She knew she would have to make time in her already overloaded schedule to address these issues.

She set up a meeting with Josh, and it went well. She laid out the problems plainly, and he seemed to grasp the message. He also seemed to understand that Jen wasn't punishing him; she was trying to help him.

Over the next several weeks, Jen met with Josh to review his progress, but his improvements came in fits and starts: a good job here, a sloppy oversight there. On some days, he seemed aware that patient welfare depended on his timeliness; on other days, he showed a disregard for the physicians and nurses waiting for his response to their requests.

UNANTICIPATED RESULTS

Jen decided she was going to try to get to the bottom of Josh's erratic progress in their next scheduled meeting. But when he showed up, he submitted his letter of resignation. Politely but nervously, he explained that he'd been offered a job with a small medical device manufacturer and had decided to accept it. He'd be starting in two weeks.

That afternoon Jen called me. She was unnerved by Josh's decision and worried that she had somehow mishandled him. She felt that she'd failed in her obligation to grow and develop this employee.

I asked Jen what specifically she had done that she regretted.

"Maybe I should have spoken to him sooner. Maybe I could have been even more explicit about the problems." Jen was grasping for answers, unconvinced that any of them really explained Josh's decision.

"How did the two of you get along through all this, Jen?"

"Really very well! That's part of the mystery. He was always responsive to my feedback and appreciative when I spoke directly and set concrete requirements. He had a nice way about him...immature and irresponsible, but something told me he had native intelligence and the potential to do better. He was easily distracted, but our business together was always cordial."

"Nothing wrong with that. But tell me, had his performance continued on its present trajectory, how would he be doing two months from now?"

Jen was now rolling the situation around in her head. "Based on the pace of his improvement from the day I started really working with him, he never would have lasted. I would have had to let him go."

"And that would have been a better outcome?" I asked incredulously.

I could tell from the pause that Jen was reconsidering her sense of failure. I tried to make the point more explicit for her.

"So let me see if I have this right: An employee isn't meeting the demands of his job. You bring it to his attention. He appreciates that you do and agrees to improve. You meet with him regularly to make sure he lives up to his word. His improvements are erratic and insufficient, but you remain supportive. Next thing you know, he resigns. And you feel responsible. I see it very differently, Jen. I think you managed this matter with unusual care and skill. Nice work."

Jen giggled and sighed at the same time. Our conversation hadn't erased her sense of disappointment. It caused her to reconsider what she was and was not responsible for. The truth is, Jen was responsible for the management *relationship*. Her task was to create a structured, supportive environment with clear requirements that would afford Josh the best chance to succeed. And she did that. But she was *not* responsible for Josh's career decision.

YARDSTICKS FOR MANAGEMENT EFFECTIVENESS

Success and failure in management are tricky things to gauge. You can't use the yardstick of a fairy tale: if the prince and princess marry and live happily ever after, it's a positive outcome; if not, it's a tragedy.

I can't overstate this point. Just think for a moment if Josh had been a more difficult person. What if he'd been more argumentative? Maybe started bad-mouthing Jen around the hospital? Maybe filed a grievance with Human Resources or a lawsuit? These certainly would not be happy developments. Josh's diversionary tactics would radically turn up the heat of the invisible spotlight. Jen would have to "manage her reputation" among her bosses, colleagues, and employees because unfounded perceptions often overrun the facts in situations like these. Most difficult, she would have to endure her *own* second-guessing.

But let's be as clear as we can on this issue: *None of Josh's maneuvers would change the fact that he was underperforming.* No matter whether he resigned because he accepted another position, or was fired for poor performance, or became combative and created all sorts of secondary distractions, Jen set a standard of performance and did not desert it. Her objective was legitimate, her execution respectful and rational. *This is what it means to fulfill your management responsibility.*

MUDDLED DEFINITIONS OF SUCCESS

For all the self-doubt that Jen felt when her employee resigned, at least his failings could be observed, defined, and communicated unambiguously. But what are you supposed to do when success and failure get muddy…when the definitions of these standards lose their sharp edges because an employee is *both* extraordinary *and* disastrous, *both* a godsend *and* your worst nightmare?

As exceptional as Susan was with her customers, that's how exasperating and destructive she was with her own colleagues.

When she was in the field servicing her software company's clients and expanding sales opportunities, Susan's enthusiasm and tenacity were unmatched. She regularly won corporate sales contests, surged past her annual bonus targets, and campaigned vigorously for improvements in the company's product line and service practices. She fully embraced the role of client advocate. When a customer called, she answered the phone or email immediately, no matter how irritating to family, friends, or colleagues. When a customer made a request, she delivered with dispatch.

In the office, Susan was unpredictable at best. When it served her purposes, she could be professional and solicitous. When things didn't go her way – when her ideas weren't greeted with immediate acceptance – she'd become dramatic, intimidating, and unreasonable. When pressures rose and the choice was between satisfying a customer on the spot or deferring to the collaborative approach preferred by her boss and colleagues – well, there really was no choice. Susan was a person who would leave bodies in her wake.

CONFLICTING MANAGEMENT IMPERATIVES

Tony, her manager, struggled with what to do. The complaints among Susan's colleagues about her arrogance and explosive outbursts were as constant as the tides. There was regular, hushed lunchroom chatter questioning why Tony was so tolerant of Susan's outlandish behavior given his earnest pitches about teamwork and company morale.

Tony counseled Susan. She would improve for short periods only to fall off the wagon. At one point, Tony established "standards of collaboration and cooperation" in her performance plan. But her miserable showing in these areas was drowned out by her sales magic.

Tony sent her to interpersonal communication classes and brought in management consultants to coach her. Susan spent most of her class time text messaging with clients. She spent most of her consultant time charming them and ignoring their counsel. She was just too smart, smug and uninterested to get much out of any of it. All the while, Susan adored her work. And year after year she made the company a boatload of money. No other salesperson could touch her numbers.

Tony's ongoing internal dialog was plagued by indecision:

> *On one hand, our clients adore her…on the other, she pushes everyone around her to their limits. We'd lose so much money and so many client contacts without*

*her…but she makes me look inept as a manager. I don't
understand why her colleagues can't just accept her
for who she is – we don't have to like each other to do
business with each other. On the other hand, all I'm
asking is that she treat her colleagues with the same
diplomacy she reserves for her clients.*

Contrary to how these thoughts might sound, they're not the
ramblings of an indecisive manager; they are the indecisive
ramblings of an anguished manager contending with two
imperatives in direct competition with one another.

Tony's first imperative was to *select the very best talent he could find*
and then provide them with whatever they needed to make
deals. The more productive his people were, the better for
them, for him, and for the company. His job was to make the
organization as profitable as he could through the talent of his
people.

Tony's second imperative was to *manage a team* – to cultivate
a professional community that worked well together. Despite
Susan's *modus operandi*, Tony's salespeople were *not* lone
rangers. Without collaboration and goodwill, *departmental*
performance was being compromised.

Susan's behavior was forcing him to choose between these
imperatives. Was her disruptive impact simply a cost of doing
business, outweighed many times over by her success in the
field? Or was that impact cancerous, slowly destroying the body
of his sales operation?

BUILDING SAFETY VALVES AND ISOLATION BOOTHS

After much thought and consultation, Tony opted for a strategy
that would let him have his cake and eat it too. He believed
his decision would enable Susan to continue delivering her

bottom-line contributions to the company and at the same time protect her colleagues from her firestorms.

Tony built a support team around her. A bulwark really. A small band of capable, hard-driving individuals assigned exclusively to Susan and her customer base. The assignment went to individuals who had expressed admiration for her aggressive style. This seemed to make things manageable. With only the occasional exception, Susan's innate arrogance and periodic outbursts were confined to a willing few. Tony once again could speak about teamwork and company spirit without eyes rolling at the hypocrisy. Department staff could function without constant fear of a brick falling on their heads.

But there were repercussions. Some of Tony's employees complained about the unfairness of Susan's private support group, insisting they could perform as well if only they had dedicated staff. And the esteem in which other employees held Tony as their manager also took a hit. Many expressed their disappointment that he'd buckled under Susan's imperiousness.

As for Tony, his eyes were wide open. He knew his employees looked to him and him alone to resolve the situation. He knew his decision was an imperfect compromise. He accurately anticipated that several of his staff would see the advantages, while others would be resentful. He prepared himself for the push-back, though he wasn't prepared for the sleepless nights over his ordeal.

Above all else, *he knew the invisible spotlight would cast some harsh and unflattering shadows.*

It always does when a decision is pragmatic and imperfect. Though the wisdom of his strategy certainly is open to vigorous debate, for the specific circumstances that Tony was navigating, this strategy was viable.

SURGERY

I have consulted with several managers confronting a dilemma strikingly similar to Tony's. One such manager chose to resolve his in a very different manner.

Over the years, Andy ran the same gauntlet with Kevin that Tony had with Susan. He counseled Kevin, established standards of conduct, tried to hide him behind intermediaries, sent him to charm school. All to no avail.

And Andy faced the same two management imperatives. He was expected to find and support the talent that would make his company as profitable as possible; and he was expected to maintain an environment in which a team of professionals could coopcrate to keep the company profitable over the long haul. But Andy reached a different conclusion:

> *Enough is enough. No one person – no matter his talents – is worth the disruption to our company's culture and to my credibility as a manager. As much as the organization may suffer in the short run by losing Kevin, and as much as I may have to pick up the slack until I replace him, we'll be better off in the long run. We'll be healthier.*

After giving Kevin one final opportunity to rein himself in – an ultimatum he just couldn't bring himself to yield to – Andy and he agreed on a separation package.

And then, like clockwork, Andy spoke the words I've learned to expect in such complicated situations, having heard them over and over again for decades:

"I should have done it sooner."

The frequency with which managers come to this same conclusion – no matter their industry, their specific position, nor the whirlwind of competing imperatives – has never ceased to astound me.

Andy had more to say some weeks later, and every word of it is instructive:

"The dark mood in the organization has lifted, our staff is more collaborative than ever, and I feel better. But make no mistake: We lost value and lots of talent when I let Kevin go. If you've never been in a job like this, you can't possibly understand what a sacrifice that is. Many close to this situation saw him only as a monster and a brute. They made him a one-dimensional caricature just so they could ignore the ambiguity of it all. But Kevin was a brilliant contributor. A money machine. He did exactly what the company is set up to do. He made our Big Guns very, very happy. And he forced us to do our best.

"Having said all this, *I should have done it sooner.*"

NO EASY WAY OUT

So many organizations have a Susan. So many of you have a Kevin. These talented, yet flawed folks offer you no easy out.

They always bring something invaluable: highly developed skills and savvy; a large black book of contacts and relationships; *gravitas* in the industry; a rare expertise; a strategic view of the company's future. And at the same time, in some other way, they are poisonous.

In these convoluted, counterweighted situations, it's important to be clear about the scope and limits of your responsibility. But it takes even more than that. *It takes a recognition – unsatisfying and inconclusive as it is – that there is no one size fits all solution. There is no black and white definition of success. No management technique applies every time. People don't always get better.*

In these situations, when there's no handbook to consult, you are left with your own assessment of the options, your own calculation of what your organization can tolerate, and your own conscience. You've done your best when you've thought these things through with care, seeking the help of those who have fought similar battles, and you're prepared to manage the consequences – both the favorable and the unfavorable ones.

Management is work. And that's in no small part because you practice it in a real and flawed world, not a world of formulas and fairy tales.

It's not only the most difficult thing to know
one's self, but the most inconvenient.

~Josh Billings

CHAPTER ELEVEN: IDIOSYNCRASIES AND IMPERFECTIONS

The knotty thing about your personal idiosyncrasies is that they're hard to recognize as a problem, yet they hold employees hostage and compromise your effectiveness

A s a manager, you bring three things to work each day:

- You bring your *mental map* of the management role – everything you've learned from role models, training programs, the reading you've done, and your own experience in leadership positions.

- You bring whatever planning and scripting you've done in preparation for the interactions you expect to have – the lines and behaviors you've worked out in your internal dialogs to make specific moments meaningful and productive.

- Finally, you bring *you* – you bring your battery of personal passions and preoccupations, preferences and prejudices, private anxieties and apprehensions, and even physical and social quirks. Sometimes these are natural gifts that will enhance your management impact; sometimes they're baggage that will burden it.

Your management relationships are profoundly affected by your virtues and idiosyncrasies. They find their way into every interaction with everyone you come in contact with: employees, colleagues, customers, vendors, bosses. And because they do, your personal watermarks not only affect the outcome of specific interactions; they define the complexion and the tempo of your entire workplace environment.

Do you remember Phil from Chapter 3? The burly trucking company district manager who justified his abusive treatment of employees by telling me, "I don't suffer fools well. That's just the way I am." That was Phil's baggage: an unmonitored, natural tendency toward impatience and insensitivity that defined him as much as his six-foot-six-inch frame. It was a destructive interpersonal quality that nearly brought him down despite his organizational successes. It controlled him rather than vice versa, and he grossly underestimated its impact.

The knotty thing about your idiosyncrasies is that they're hands down the hardest realities for you to recognize as a problem. Idiosyncrasies are personal; so much a part of us that we've grown blind to them. We've lived with our quirks for as long as we've lived with our selves. If they're brought to our attention (and they rarely are), we have a ready arsenal of justifications and defenses because we prefer to keep them out of sight.

What we don't realize is that we're far better at hiding unflattering baggage from ourselves than from everyone else.

It's no surprise then, that you assume these parts of your character have no impact on your management relationships. But make no mistake: in the same way your employees benefit from your personal virtues and healthy management behaviors, they're held hostage by your foibles. And, for the most part, they suffer in silence.

Let's look at a few examples from the infinite variety offered by human nature. Then I'll discuss where and how you can find the mirrors that reflect your own idiosyncrasies; how you can discipline yourself to look at what's in them without flinching;

and how you can protect your management relationships from the damage that unnoticed habits can inflict.

PEEVISHNESS

A senior official in a large nonprofit organization once described to me a four-minute conversation that opened his eyes to the impact of personal imperfections.

Calvin had established excellent relationships with his co-workers and employees. He was widely recognized for having improved the organization's social services to some of the most neglected populations in the country. He was respected for his commitment to the underprivileged as well as his ability to bring noble ideas to ground level so real human beings could actually benefit from them.

Early one morning, he received a call from Jackie, the VP of research and program evaluation, to coordinate a meeting for later that day. From Calvin's perspective, the conversation was perfunctory. He gave it half-minded attention, agreed with her suggestions for the agenda, and got back to his paperwork as soon as he hung up the phone.

Moments later, Jackie appeared at Calvin's door and asked tersely, "Do we have a problem?" She explained she had sensed impatience in his voice and wanted to make certain there were no subterranean gremlins between them. Obviously her concern was of such magnitude that she wasted no time making the commute from three floors below.

Calvin, though bewildered, began assuring her that he was unaware of any friction. Then he stopped midsentence as a memory intruded. He smiled sheepishly. "Jackie, my thirteen-year-old daughter took my wife and me through the ringer this morning in ways that only a thirteen-year-old girl can. If remnants of that firestorm are lingering in my voice, I apologize." Calvin was plainly embarrassed. "I'm sorry I didn't keep it under better control, but please know that you and I are fine." They exhaled in unison, and Jackie left the office, letting Calvin off the hook with a compassionate smile.

He hadn't told her the whole truth, though. While Calvin's impatience that morning was in fact the residue of a breakfast spat with his daughter, this wasn't the first time the testiness beneath his otherwise calm demeanor had bled through. In fact, his wife, children, and close friends had called him out for years on his "peevish tone of voice." Until the incident with Jackie, however, he was confident he had it camouflaged at work. Now he had his doubts.

For days, Calvin couldn't get the conversation with Jackie out of his mind. He was forced to see how attuned she and his other colleagues were to his moods. If she could detect his irritation in a brief and inconsequential phone call, he probably was sending countless signals throughout the day without realizing it. That the issue was now consuming so much of his mental energy told him he could no longer ignore it.

He began to think about his employees, especially those who had neither the fortitude nor the organizational standing to call him on his rudeness. If he was going to rein in this aspect of his behavior, he couldn't rely on them to act as a check and balance. He would have to do that himself. Calvin knew the impatience Jackie had unmasked was a quality that also drove him to be successful. He would have to be ever mindful that it drove others to distraction. His burning desire to succeed singed others when it neared the surface.

Jackie was a colleague, and a forthright one at that. She was sensitive to "atmospherics" and self-possessed enough to confront him on the meaning of his behavior. Calvin had enough self-awareness to take seriously the breach of composure that she detected. It was a happy but rare confluence of candor and wisdom that was a turning point in the way he managed. More often, managers drift in a fog of inattention when it comes to their personal and emotional junk. They can't count on their employees to hold up a mirror.

POLITICAL SABOTAGE

Rick loved politics. He enjoyed taking strong views on many of the more divisive social and political issues of the day. He often laced his political views into his directives, conversations, and observations. What began innocently enough as friendly teasing and give-and-take with his employees degenerated over time into an uncomfortable separation of those who agreed with Rick's politics, those who held opposing views, and those who couldn't care less.

Because of the atmosphere he established, his employees walked on eggshells with little or no place to take refuge. Take a position counter to Rick's? Probably not in your best interest to argue with your boss. Take no point of view and appear indifferent? Who wants to go to work and cower all day? How about stating that it's inappropriate to discuss politics at work? Sounds good, but isn't that like telling your boss he has body odor?

Rick's people came to feel threatened by the intensity of his interest in their political positions. It began to overshadow the work at hand. His obsession with politics became an intrusion they had to step over, hide from, and maneuver around to get to the work they were hired to do.

Unlike Calvin, Rick had no Jackie. His was a personal preoccupation run amok. What's important to note here is that, from a strictly technical standpoint, Rick was a reasonably good manager. His employees got their work done, they were pleasant enough for outsiders to interact with, they were experienced and knowledgeable. Rick's bosses were pleased enough with his unit that they could turn their attention elsewhere in the organization where there were "real" problems.

But *how would you like to be working for Rick?* What would your workday be like? How would you answer when your spouse asked how your day went? Rick illustrates the harmful influence of a manager's idiosyncrasies when they infiltrate relationships unchecked. Calvin was made aware of what the invisible spotlight was revealing and resolved to make a change. Rick had no idea he needed to.

CHEST BEATING

Tom was a company man. He drove himself to advance his standing in his organization and in life. At the beginning of his career, his motivation seemed a healthy desire to get ahead. He was willing to pay his dues. He applied for positions that would round out his experience, often requiring his family to relocate every few years. His resume was expanding, as were his competence and value to the organization.

But that wasn't enough for Tom. It was becoming more and more important to him that his contributions and his promise not be overlooked. Somewhere in the recesses of his mind, he had a timetable for his advancement, and that timetable controlled his every move.

As a result, Tom made certain that those with whom he interacted were aware of his value. His capacity to link his contributions to company successes – even those that were far removed from his base of influence – was at first clever:

> "I happened to have been instrumental in encouraging the president to make that big change."

> "My groundwork with a few key customers and prospects made it possible for that department to land the contract."

> "I made that very point during a conference in Cincinnati three years ago."

Over time, the predictability of his peacocking became comical and eventually pathetic.

His employees were embarrassed by his self-promotion, fearing that his behavior was a reflection on them. Tom's self-aggrandizement, and the personal insecurity that it betrayed, eventually became a hindrance to their work and their own advancement.

Here again, we see a manager with no clue. Tom, like the rest of us, had lived with his preoccupation for as long as he'd lived with himself. He had little capacity to look at it from the outside in, and no boss, employee, colleague, consultant, training program, or management book was holding up a mirror. He had no idea what he looked like under the unseen spotlight.

INDIFFERENCE

Some managers see their management role as an inconvenience, like taking out the garbage. It's got to be done, but it's hard to put your heart into it. These managers don't commit many errors; they simply don't commit.

The personal flaw in this case can come from many places: negative social experiences early in life; early management situations that didn't go well; a voracious interest in other aspects of work that leaves no room for the management task; a focus on only the procedural aspects of the management role.

Vivian fit this mold. She worked hard but was largely uninterested in her management obligations. She liked working without interruption and preferred her door closed. She often neglected to greet her staff in the hallways. She kept her meetings to a minimum. She was annoyed and vaguely bemused by how needy her employees seemed to be.

Before her promotion to management, Vivian didn't need a lot of care and feeding. In fact, her self-directedness was one of the primary reasons her bosses saw management potential in her. Unfortunately, Vivian managed her staff as if they were her. She saw no need to communicate beyond the minimum. The work was assigned, the schedules developed, the progress monitored and documented, the work completed, and new work assigned. All good, except that many of her employees needed more. Some were accustomed to a bigger picture. Others needed a little more time to understand this or that approach. Still others simply needed more explicit assurances that their contributions were valued.

Vivian wasn't doing wrong. She just wasn't doing right. Her values, preferences, and anxieties controlled her minimalist management behavior. As a manager, Vivian mattered to her employees. But it didn't seem to matter to her that she did.

NEEDINESS

Jack loved his work and enjoyed his position as director of special projects. He had a contagious enthusiasm that encouraged his employees to be productive and imaginative. Jack liked people and liked having them around him. He actually loved the spotlight and didn't care whether it was the invisible one or a real one!

As a result Jack called a lot of meetings. At first this was heady stuff for his staff – to be called into their director's conference room made them feel important and valued. Jack would often have these meetings catered, and if not, there was always an assortment of soft drinks, coffee, and teas. He knew how to make people feel important. But his meetings began to be an interference. They were often called at a moment's notice, and even more often had vague purposes and a questionable agenda.

Jack's frequent meetings eventually lead to extended lunches, then weekend golf outings, then get-togethers at his home. Jack was taking advantage of his authority to gratify a personal need. He was engineering moments in his management relationships, but the moments were not serving business ends. Jack couldn't see this.

Like Rick and Tom and Vivian, Jack had no internal barometer. No way of gauging his impact. And nothing in his environment was pinching him to notice. So it was only natural and human for him to mistake his employees' attentiveness for respect and admiration. When you're a boss like Jack, your employees will laugh at your jokes, agree with your ideas, express gratitude for your hospitality and generosity. These superficial gestures will obscure the reality of discomfort and resentment beneath them.

BEWARE OF AUTOPILOT

You're on managerial autopilot when your own passions, preoccupations, and prejudices contaminate your management relationships, and everyone knows it but you.

The list of annoyances and irritations managers carry unknowingly into their jobs is as varied as managers are. I suspect you too have heard employees and colleagues complain:

> "He talks too much; his explanations go on and on."

> "She's distracted by the least little thing and she can't stay on topic."

> "He's too fearful to make a decision."

> "All she does is sit in her office."

> "The only time we see any life in her is when her boss visits the floor."

Every one of us carries our idiosyncrasies into our work. When we're responsible for the lives and livelihoods of others, what we carry affects many more people than ourselves.

Typically the only recourse for employees trapped by their boss's quirks and preoccupations is to commiserate among themselves in lunch rooms and carpools and on out-of-town trips. This is precisely why the problem is insidious and self-perpetuating. You receive no feedback on these things. There's no mirror to look into. A manager flies on autopilot because a manager *can* fly on autopilot. *Nothing in the jet steam forces him to grab the manual controls and correct his course.*

THE SELF-OBSERVANT MANAGER

The observant manager studies himself – often and intensively. In the same way he checks his body for skin irregularities that might become cancerous, he periodically asks his bosses, colleagues and employees how he's doing. Sometimes he asks directly, sometimes more subtly. Sometimes it's awkward, sometimes it's halting, and sometimes it's enormously illuminating. Often it creates its own pivotal moment in the management relationship. When there is no one to ask, he asks himself by turning his observing ego inward.

Beyond this feedback, self-observant managers seek assessments of their management behavior from sources beyond the immediate workplace. They take classes that include individual evaluations and 360-degree feedback from employees, colleagues, and superiors. They talk with an impartial consultant or counselor who will provide an unvarnished critique. They read about the common pitfalls that managers fall into unawares. They study managers whom they admire and those whose flaws they want to avoid.

Self-observant managers are keenly aware that they're in the pilot's seat. They are unwilling to let the aircraft do its own thing. They know if the foundation of the management relationship is solid, they are doing something right. If it fails or falters, they are doing something wrong.

It takes a lot of character to control your behavior. It's a different order of magnitude than learning a new mechanical skill, managing a concrete situation, or incorporating a new, organizationwide management program. The only way to optimize your best parts and quiet your most problematic ones is to turn off autopilot from time to time and consciously, deliberately maneuver the controls yourself.

Rank does not confer privilege or give power. It imposes responsibility.

~Peter Drucker

CHAPTER TWELVE: MANAGING MANAGERS

It falls to you to sensitize your managers to the invisible spotlight — where it shines, who's in the audience watching, how long the show goes on, how a manager performs in it

L et's return for a moment to Phil, our brawny district manager from chapter 3.

Phil's turnaround of the district's performance was nothing short of outstanding. In the span of one year, he transformed a dysfunctional organization into a profitable machine. While this was exactly what his company hoped he would achieve, no one expected so dramatic a reversal of fortune in so short a time.

Phil's bare-knuckled approach to his management relationships, however, humiliated and alienated his employees and troubled his boss. Though Phil applied himself and ultimately learned new and better ways to navigate those management relationships, he was certainly not the hero of our story. His employees risked untold repercussions by discussing their dilemmas, fears, and frustrations with an outsider, but they weren't the heroes either. And neither was the consultant who held up a mirror that reflected Phil's imperfections.

In fact, the hero of that saga was Phil's boss, Stuart, the vice president of operations.

Here was a guy who could have sat back and basked in the quarter-over-quarter improvements that were streaming in from the Cleveland District. He could have delighted in the accolades from the central office for his prescient choice of management talent. He could have looked forward to a handsome bonus at the end of the year for masterminding a stunning success.

Stuart could have disregarded the indications that all was not well in the Cleveland District, ignoring the complaints coming into the human resources department and dismissing as collateral damage the loss of district supervisors who quit rather than continue under Phil's iron rule. After all, you can't make an omelet without breaking a few eggs.

Over time, Stuart might have watched Phil self-destruct and then replaced him with a less demanding manager who employees would better relate to. He could have hoped that Phil's countless operational improvements would carry the district for several more quarters before the inevitable backslide.

Fortunately for Phil, his VP had a longer and more enlightened view. Stuart subscribed to the philosophy that the respectful, civil treatment of subordinates is every bit as important as short-term financial success. In fact, our hero believed a supportive environment made long-term prosperity *far more likely*. He was convinced that, without a satisfied workforce, Phil's district was a house of cards.

Within a week after my first visit to Cleveland, Stuart traveled to the district to talk with Phil face to face. He took the time to explain three things:

1. As far as Stuart was concerned, while a manager might achieve short-term successes through intimidation, long-term success requires that people be treated with dignity, that they be made to feel a part of the organization and respected for their contributions.

2. Phil's operational and economic effectiveness was impressive but not sufficient. While the company placed a high value on Cleveland's performance, Phil would also be evaluated on the quality of his management relationships.

3. It would be challenging for Phil to make meaningful improvements. Stuart understood that impatience and an authoritarian instinct were embedded in Phil's character and in fact made much of his rapid success in Cleveland possible. He nonetheless had confidence in Phil's capacity for self-reflection and development and would support that development with training, consultation, and a continuing dialog between them.

Phil had come to work for this company right out of school. In all his years moving up through the ranks, no superior had ever set this priority. At moments in the conversation, Phil was confused. He felt like Stuart was asking him to babysit, not lead; he had trouble grasping his VP's idea that the means were as important as the ends.

By the time the conversation was over, Phil was clearer on the message. After all, in the span of one week, he'd heard it from the consultant, then the boss. But the message made him anxious. It meant he'd no longer be able to excuse himself by saying, "This is just the way I am."

A MANAGEMENT PHILOSOPHY

Interestingly, Phil wasn't the only one surprised by the exchange. Stuart surprised himself, too. The episode was a milestone for both men's professional development.

While Stuart always believed instinctively that the welfare of employees was basic to a sustainable workplace, it had never coalesced as part of his conscious management philosophy. While it was something he brought to his own dealings with employees, it never before dawned on him that he had both the right and the obligation to demand it from the managers who reported to him. He hadn't realized that his personal priority was also a coherent and legitimate management philosophy.

He said much later, "I had never been as clear with any manager or management team as I was that day with Phil. I'd never before said that treating employees with dignity is a management imperative. Pure and simple. I told Phil, 'If you can't learn to do it, I don't want you on my team.' It felt right when I said it, and it's felt right ever since."

MANAGEMENT BY DEMONSTRATION

Let's be clear. Phil didn't improve as a manager because of some deep moral sense or because he suddenly got in touch with his softer side. He didn't improve because of his consultant's luminous insights and recommendations. As much as the conversation with his VP was a watershed moment for both of them, Phil didn't make authentic improvements in his management relationships because of that *single* conversation. Maybe, as time passed, he realized some of the benefits of a more gracious demeanor. But in those uncertain early days following Stuart's visit, all Phil could do was try to grasp what his vice president wanted and then try to do it.

Ultimately, Phil altered his approach to management because he *didn't want to lose his job*. It was that simple. But there was also this: Stuart didn't just preach good management, he practiced it. He didn't just spout a management philosophy; he demonstrated it in his own interactions with Phil and with others. This was not lost on Phil. While the threat of losing his job got Phil to clean up his act, Stuart showed him *how to do it*. Stuart, as they say, "walked the talk" – not a new management concept, but never so important as when you're managing managers and the issue at hand is *how they're managing*!

Do you remember the "Caring Culture" fiasco in chapter 7? Let me remind you of one of the important lessons from that scenario:

No matter how artfully you orchestrate a given interaction, it alone won't ensure the success of your management relationships. You're in the invisible spotlight between interactions, too. During these periods, your employees are looking for signs of your credibility. They're judging if you mean what you say. They're comparing word and deed. They're following your lead, not just your lips.

STRAIGHT TALK ABOUT IDIOSYNCRASIES

When Janice was first hired as an executive with a large, aeronautical design firm, she made an important discovery about the value of management philosophies. As with many discoveries, this one was born of dissatisfaction and concern.

Janice was impressed with the managers she'd inherited. To a person, they were formidable – experienced, well credentialed, accomplished in their specialties, and passionate about the firm's contributions to aerospace equipment and technologies. Janice herself was no lightweight; she'd trained at an excellent university, worked on a wide array of projects with a number of design firms around the world, and held her own with intelligence and grace in a proverbial man's world. Nonetheless, her current direct reports were clearly an imposing breed.

Yet for all their virtues, they posed some problems that disturbed Janice a lot.

Bob was a hothead whose explosive outbursts at the slightest provocation were renowned throughout his department. His staff was cowed and tentative.

Harvey repeatedly made cynical and unwarranted asides about "ridiculous client requirements" and "repressive internal policies" that made any new corporate initiative a trial. His employees were known to be obstructionist and rebellious.

Diana was icy in manner and could be difficult when working on technical or organizational problems, certain as she was that the problems others identified were either fictions or easily resolved her way. She provided little guidance to her staff, who were often confused and inefficient.

Janice viewed these managers as her professional equals – it was the unspoken culture within the industry, to minimize the "above/below" nature of management relationships and regard each other as colleagues. She also considered her managers indispensable experts – so vital to the firm's work that their loss would have a devastating organizational impact and be a personal failure.

As a result, she was loath to raise her concerns about their stylistic idiosyncrasies, fearful of running them off. In her mind, their character foibles were off limits. Whenever she envisioned a conversation with one of her managers, her internal dialogs always ended badly, with the manager in a huff: "Listen, I've been doing this a long time." "I have a successful track record." "Why are we discussing these trivial irrelevancies about management?" "Why don't you just let me do my job?"

THE INTERNAL DIALOG

Janice was being held hostage by her managers' reputations and technical competence and by her own misperception that she was merely first among equals rather than the boss. On the other hand, she knew the climate within her department was unnecessarily unhealthy. As the evidence mounted that employees were being ill served and mistreated, she landed on a conclusion:

Yes, these managers are gifted experts, expected to use their expertise in the service of their jobs. But I too have been hired here to use my expertise – both my technical and my managerial expertise. I've seen enough in my career to know what a healthy and productive management relationship should look like. These relationships don't measure up. This firm is legitimately entitled to both excellent results and excellent management.

The insight enabled Janice to rework her internal dialogs. In turn, her insight was the impetus for a series of uncomfortable exchanges with her managers in which she kept returning to her management philosophy:

> "I will let you do your job, but not at the expense of your employees' dignity and pride, both of which are suffering now. This firm is not merely an organization set up to deliver goods and services. It's also a human community in which mutual respect and common decency are mandatory. And by the way, if you can learn to see the value of your management relationships, you'll elevate the quality of our designs over the long haul!"

Janice discovered that once she made this fundamental expectation clear to her managers (and to herself), she suddenly felt at liberty to communicate her specific observations and deliver some feedback.

> "Bob, when you get pressured, you get mean. Not with me – you're always pleasant with me – but with your folks. Getting mad is easy, but it's unacceptable. Lighten up, stay in control. Your people need your levelheadedness as much I do...."

"Harvey, I know you take considerable pleasure in the maverick role. It's fun for you to shoot at corporate targets. Here's the thing, though: it's become predictable. Everyone knows the posture you'll take before you take it. You give the impression that you haven't even considered the merits of this or that requirement or policy; you'll reload just because it *is* a requirement or policy. I wonder if you're aware of the impact this has on your staff. I wonder if you can see that they're often silenced by your knee-jerk cynicism rather than energized. You make it very difficult for them to work as part of the team, even if they want to. Well, I want them to be free to work as part of the team. By all means, shoot holes when it's warranted. But shoot them with discretion and discrimination. Don't cripple your employees in the process. It will certainly make it more worthwhile for all of us to listen to what you have to say...."

"Diana, I know it's not in your nature to schmooze. You're all business, and it's served both you and the work of this firm. But your employees are almost entirely out of the loop. Your failure to lay out your plans and expectations for them, your refusal to solicit their ideas, your intolerance for problems they may be having – these are creating an unacceptably isolating and unfulfilling environment for them. And you're getting much less out of them than they have to offer. Reversing this atmosphere is as much your obligation as meeting deadlines, staying within budgets, complying with technical specifications...."

For Janice, these discussions were painful. She also believed they were unavoidable. In each, she made plain that she wasn't so arrogant as to try to change personalities. She wasn't trying to play Dr. Phil. She wasn't trying to unearth how her managers came to be the way they were. She was trying to create an organizational environment in which management relationships are valued and managers are conscious of how much their impact matters.

She had formidable egos to contend with. When it got down to her drawing a line in the sand in each of these conversations, her approach resembled a renowned movie director's: After patiently explaining to his star actress the nuances of her character's response in a scene, the actress continued to complain that she "just wasn't feeling it." The director smiled and said, "Darling, you're an actress. Fake it." Words to live by. We all have to learn to act the part sometimes.

MANAGEMENT TRAINING AND DEVELOPMENT

As part of their resolve to elevate the quality of management in their organizations, both Stuart and Janice encouraged their direct reports to attend classroom management training. This is a common recourse. Maybe the most common. But neither Stuart nor Janice was under the misconception that formal training programs *in and of themselves* will have much impact. Learning the complexities and subtleties of management is akin to learning a new language.

Classrooms can only drill on the fundamentals; they provide ideals and abstractions. Real fluency with an unfamiliar tongue is achieved when it's practiced every day in an environment that requires it. This is where both Stuart and Janice came in. They explained what they wanted and modeled for their managers how they expected the job to be done. This is where you come in, too. You have to do what you want your people to do.

Your own expectations for management excellence must be on the table. Explicitly and unambiguously. Naturally, the very best time to put them there is from the start – when you're first taking the helm, or when a manager is first joining your team. But *any* time is the right time when a manager reporting to you is falling short. These are the moments in which you set the most influential and enduring precedents.

You must be willing to inquire about your managers' relationships with their employees – discuss them in some detail; critique them as if they are as central to the work as anything else; offer strategies for creating constructive moments and handling uncomfortable moments with employees; recognize improvements when your managers make them. If need be, you must even be willing to assign tasks to your managers that are specifically designed to test and improve their skills.

It falls to you to sensitize your managers to the invisible spotlight – where it shines, who's in the audience watching, how long the show goes on, how a manager performs in it. In other words, you must create a culture in which management excellence is valued and publicly rewarded in the same way other business achievements are. This establishes management effectiveness as an organizational priority.

Most important, you must demonstrate every day what you're asking your managers to strive for. This is the *sine qua non* of management development – the single most important condition for promoting management excellence.

When these conditions are met, classroom training can make a contribution to your managers' development. If this sounds a lot like what you would do with your children when you send them to an expensive tutor, you're right, it is. We are all pigeons, children, employees, and managers.

Your managers learn when you place a premium on what they're supposed to learn. You have the greatest effect when you take an interest in it and have the courage to tell them when they're not measuring up and when they are. This principle may never be so important as when you're in a position to manage managers.

Look at all the sentences which
seem true and question them.

~David Riesmen

CLOSING THOUGHTS

Now that we come to our conclusion, allow us to return to being the "we" that we two authors really are.

Throughout this book, we've dissected the management relationship from all angles. With dozens of scenarios and observations, we've tried to make the invisible spotlight *visible* so you could appreciate the many ways to create a foundation for your management relationships and the great value of doing so.

Our consulting work over the past thirty-five years with countless managers has convinced us of this: once you see how closely your words and deeds are scrutinized by your employees and how significant your impact is on their lives, you'll begin to manage your important moments of interaction with them more wisely and deliberately. You'll also avoid many of the hazards of working in the dark.

We've said it's the *moments* that matter. Now *of course* you should try to cultivate a management "style." And *of course* you should put in place the most up-to-date management systems and controls. But management actually *happens* in moments – those fleeting opportunities that you're so prone to overlook. What you say and don't say, what you do and don't do *in the moment* determine how firm the foundation of your management relationships will be.

Your behavior in the moment can cause your employees hours of uncertainty and distress, or it can heighten their commitment and contribution in a profound and lasting way. Without meaningful moments, your management style is stilted and inauthentic, and management systems are antiseptic and without a soul.

As we mentioned in our introduction, some of the lessons in these pages probably have made immediate sense to you; they reflect your own experience and outlook. Others have forced you to think differently about the management role. Still others may make sense only with time and further reflection. Regardless of if, when, and how our ideas find their way into your thinking and day-to-day actions, what we've tried to convey is that mastering the management relationship doesn't ensure organizational success; it increases the likelihood that you'll get the maximum out of your employees and your organization. Do it well and you become a more significant factor in positive organizational outcomes. Do it poorly or mindlessly or not at all and you become a negative influence on those outcomes.

AN HONORABLE PROFESSION

The magical thing about managing in an unseen spotlight is that your employees – your audience – very much *want* you to be good. They *want* you to be effective. They're *rooting* for you to be successful. This is because *their* lives are made immeasurably easier, more predictable, and more rewarding if you manage your relationships deliberately and honorably. Your employees can be energized, even inspired by how well you perform. This is how powerful your impact can be. This is how much you matter.

The stories and scenarios in this book illustrate a wide variety of day-to-day moments – some dramatic and pivotal, others mundane and fleeting – in which your management relationships will be strengthened or compromised. Which way these moments go depends on a few things: your willingness to act in unnatural and unfamiliar ways to achieve a clear and productive result; the time you take to anticipate and choreograph important moments; the premium you place on preserving a candid and mutually respectful relationship regardless of the subject or task at hand; and your commitment to self-observation, self-reflection, and self-improvement. In other words the success of your relationships requires that you relentlessly assess how your important moments have gone, why they went the way they did, what needs to happen next, and how they can be better handled next time. The point is *you are the architect* of these moments of interaction.

> *If the foundation of the management relationship is solid, you're doing something right. If it falters or fails, you're doing something wrong. It's that simple and that difficult.*

Management is hard work. It involves complexities that can't be simplified. It is an honorable profession that demands thoughtfulness and wisdom and ethical considerations beyond step-by-step recipes. So if we've gotten you to *think* differently about the way you perform your role and manage your relationships, we'll count it as a success.

Tomorrow you'll be back in the office. We hope you'll welcome the heat of the invisible spotlight, the weight of your management relationships, the honor of your profession. We hope you'll embrace how much you matter to the people who are most dependent on you for their sense of self-worth and success.

ACKNOWLEDGMENTS

All books are collaborations, and this one is no exception. While we assume full responsibility for its content, many people have graciously given their time and attention to improve its clarity and quality. Though their candor has sometimes punctured our vain pretensions to substantive brilliance and a literary flair, it has in every instance been deeply appreciated.

In particular, for their critical reading of the manuscript at various points in its development, we thank Dr. Alan Leshner, Vic Morgenstern, Steve Farris, Dean Woods, Lisa Stewart, Elaine Kurtz, Susan Herman, Cherise Burdeen, Kregg Olsen, Zoe Beinart, Fred Synder, Donna Triptow Salzberry, Eric Williamson, Michael Feldman, Fred Gardner, Steve Green, Peter Tuters, Becky Hoyt, Daryl Kenningham, Tom Bittenbender, Chris Pavelocick, Mike Owen, Dr. Stuart Grauer, Patrick Burns, Laura Ryan, Bill Katz, Jason Katz, Chad Braverman, Jarret Stuhl and Stacy Shappro.

Several people went well beyond customary courtesy and generosity. They read the manuscript with the greatest attention to detail, sometimes more than once, and offered specific, constructive suggestions that immeasurably improved the book's message and presentation We owe Kathleen Wasserman, Karen Orlansky, Cornell Jaray, Michael Osterman, and Jeff Parent a special debt of gratitude.

At times this project consumed so much of our energy that the ones we love were squeezed out. So finally, we want to thank our families for their many invaluable, substantive contributions as well as their tolerance for the endless thinking, talking, writing, fighting and playing of best friends trying to codify what they've learned from a lifetime of consulting. To our wives, Kathleen and Kathy, and our children, Lizzie and Victor Wasserman, and Jamie and Malory Katz, we thank you for reading our book and reading our minds and hearts. We dedicate this book to you.

THE AUTHORS

CRAIG W. WASSERMAN, Ph.D.

As a management consultant, trainer and lecturer since 1976, Craig has left consultant-speak behind to focus in common sense ways on the uneasy, unfamiliar moments that managers encounter as they develop relationships with their employees. He helps managers explore their ultimate responsibility for making these critical organizational relationships work.

Craig earned his degrees from American University in Washington, D.C.: a Bachelor of Science in Organizational Development, a Master of Education in Counseling, and a Doctor of Philosophy in Counseling Psychology. He followed these studies with a year's Post Doctoral Internship at the University of Maryland, and immediately cofounded Wasserman/Katz. He took a two and a half year sabbatical from the firm to work as Vice President, Human Resources and Organizational Development at Browning Ferris Industries.

Today Craig splits his time between Steamboat Springs, Colorado and Houston, Texas with Kathleen, his wife of twenty seven years.

DOUG KATZ, M.A.

For almost four decades, Doug has been advising managers on the most intelligent ways to steward their organizations and navigate their relationships with employees and colleagues.

In addition to his direct consulting work from California to Washington, DC, Doug is often retained to facilitate meetings and conferences addressing controversial issues affecting an organization or community. He has been involved in a fifteen year study of national labor and employment trends to help his clients prepare for emerging workforce challenges. He was a guest instructor on Business Ethics in the University of Maryland's Honors Program from 2002-2006 and has served on the Boards of The Grauer School, the Pretrial Justice Institute, IDC Marketing, Inc., Red Shark Technology, and The Woolly Mammoth Theater Company.

JamArtz (jamartz.com) is a branding and communication design studio, an outgrowth of Wasserman/Katz that Doug launched in 1990. Having grown up in a New York City advertising family, and having worked as a fashion and product photographer in a New York agency, Doug uses his commercial illustration, design, and copywriting skills to serve the needs of some of Wasserman/Katz's clients. The studio now stands on its own, creating identity systems, marketing copy and collateral, fundraising communications, poster art, signage, and editorial illustration for local, regional and national clients.

Doug earned Bachelor of Arts and Master of Arts degrees in Clinical Psychology from American University in Washington, DC. He was awarded an NIMH Clinical Training Fellowship and an NIMH Research Assistantship. He completed a clinical internship, upon graduation served as an editorial consultant with a publisher of academic texts, and soon after co-founded Wasserman/Katz. Doug lives in San Diego, California with his wife of thirty five years.

To purchase additional copies of this book, visit:

www.amazon.com

To learn more about the authors or to contact them directly, visit:

www.wassermankatz.com

www.theinvisiblespotlight.com